# LET US BUILD US A CITY

# Let Us Build Us a City

TRACY DAUGHERTY

The University of Georgia Press   *Athens*

© 2017 by the University of Georgia Press
Athens, Georgia 30602
www.ugapress.org
All rights reserved
Designed by Erin Kirk New
Set in Minion Pro
Printed and bound by Thomson-Shore
The paper in this book meets the guidelines for
permanence and durability of the Committee on
Production Guidelines for Book Longevity of the
Council on Library Resources.

Most University of Georgia Press titles are
available from popular e-book vendors.

Printed in the United States of America
21  20  19  18  17  P  5  4  3  2  1

Library of Congress Control Number: 2016958182
ISBN: 9780820350813 (paperback: alk. paper)
ISBN: 9780820350806 (ebook)

*For Margie, for Rosellen Brown,*

*and in memory of Ehud Havazelet*

# CONTENTS

# LET US BUILD US A CITY

# Introduction

*The Falling-in-Love*

In the *Convivio*, a book left unfinished for reasons no one knows, Dante says a person should not write or speak of himself except under extraordinary circumstances: a) when "great disgrace and danger cannot be avoided" without self-reference, or b) when "great advantage to others" may be had.

I won't claim this book's occasion reflects either of these circumstances, but Dante's conviction reminds me that those of us who dabble in fiction often stress that our works have little to do with our lives. We make this claim not to refute the words we've inscribed but to slant our words away from us. Most writers' preferred location is the periphery, quietly taking notes so as to accurately render what we see. It's hard to take sensible measure of a place when *you* become the center of attention. Dante understood this. His advice springs from a pragmatic as well as an ethical core: the best material is *out there* somewhere, beyond the mirror. Individually, none of us is ever more important than the world around us.

That said, and with all due respect to our greatest poet, I confess that a character in a recent story of mine echoes my sentiments when he says, "Periodically, most professionals seek a renewal. A return to first principles. When the business starts to feel stale or the ideas dry up, we try to remember what drew us to our work in the first place—that initial euphoria, the falling-in-love."

Preparing these essays, meditating on the literary imagination and the craft behind it, has provided me an opportunity to reflect on how I first fell in love with what I do. In the spirit of Dante, these reflections center initially on those around me: family, friends, and colleagues. No

1

individual is remotely capable apart from community, and I have been blessed with an unusually patient and supportive family, at home and at the institutions where I have taught literature and writing.

In institutional life (where, for better or worse, most literary practitioners find their home in America these days), we speak of "collegiality." The word means many things. My training, as a student of the humanities in institutions of higher learning, inclines me to look first at the human subtext of any definition, so for me, to be colleagues means to grow old with one another. Whatever you do for a living, wherever you work, next time you're attending a meeting with colleagues, headsore from competing agendas, unfocused discussion, and bureaucratic roadblocks, look around the room at the folks sitting next to you and consider: "These are the people with whom I am growing old."

This perspective brings a melancholy chill but it also offers comfort; it contextualizes our daily tasks, reduces everything to first principles and the oh-so-human. It reminds us that everything we do as individuals and as colleagues is complex and mysterious and always shifting, and I'm grateful to have been able to share the mysteries of life, writing, and teaching with superlative partners. Because of them, I have been able to gather and develop the thoughts behind these essays.

Besides prompting self-examination, attempts at renewal always involve reappraisals of one's specialty—in my case, literature; specifically, American literature but with an eye on Europe and in developments in all the arts—and I've found it useful, lately, to return to a book that spells out what it means to live a literary life in this country.

The book is Susan Cheever's *Home before Dark*.

The novelist and short story writer John Cheever provided a literary model for many writers of my generation. In rereading his daughter's memoir of him, I am reminded that he arrived in Manhattan in 1930, penniless and alone, determined to succeed in the great city like so many writers before him. He rented a room on Hudson Street for three dollars a week and began composing the first of the stories that are today widely anthologized and read. According to Susan, he struggled for twenty-five years to write his first novel. In 1978, his third novel, *Falconer*, as well as *The Collected Stories of John Cheever* won him fame and lasting recognition.

Apparently, he had not heard Dante on humility, because suddenly "he seemed to be his own number one groupie," Susan recalls. "Conversations with him often resorted to discussions of his own success, his celebrity, and the way Lauren (Betty) Bacall had ardently kissed him the last time they met."

At the height of this success, Cheever came to Dallas, Texas, for a literary festival, a week of readings and panel discussions, at Southern Methodist University. I was a teaching assistant there, an eager writing student, and festival cochair. My job was to escort Cheever wherever he wanted to go—a local bakery, where he ate free pastries and donned a paper chef's hat; the Amon Carter Museum in Fort Worth, where he marveled at Frederick Remington's paintings of American deserts. "I'm grateful for this steady autumn sun," he told me quietly one morning as though confessing a vice. He was amazed that two cities the size of Dallas and Fort Worth could have developed so closely together. "What are their economies based on? Is there much political infighting between them?" he asked me. Ignorant of business and sociopolitics, I had no answers for him but noted, These are the kinds of things a writer worries about.

I had no idea how to engage this man whose achievements set an impossibly high standard for my own pale efforts. At one point, a swift red car passed us on a freeway. "That's the color of your book of stories," I said, a comment so inane it deserved no response. "Yes, it is," he said, looking pleased. "Yes, it is."

He made a point of addressing each student he met by name and spoke to us all as though we were friends. All week, despite his recent accolades, he appeared less than modest only once, when he discovered that Louis Simpson, another festival guest, had won a Pulitzer Prize in 1964. For an hour or so, Cheever ignored Simpson. He had thought *he* was the only prize-winner present.

One night, toward the festival's close, an English professor held a small dinner party in his Craftsman-style home, a cramped place with wooden floors, massive square furnishings, volumes of Freud and Lionel Trilling on the shelves. Candles were lit and Cheever held forth in front of the hearth, waving a cup of ginger ale. He said he'd given up liquor for Lent (in fact, though none of us knew it then, he'd stopped drinking, with great anguish, in 1975). Someone asked him what else he'd given up. He smiled. His skin, still supple at sixty-seven, folded over the grand, rolling bones in his cheeks. "Well," he said, turning in every direction, mischievously eyeing each person in the room. "My cock fell off at Easter."

A writer is charming, I said to myself.

The following afternoon, I moderated a symposium featuring Cheever, Simpson, a young writer named David Huddle, and my writing teacher, Marsh Terry. I was terrified, especially since Simpson, whose manner was sharp, had taken a seat next to mine on the dais. My first question was, "Is it possible to come up with original literary forms now, or has everything been done?"

Simpson turned to me disdainfully. "Every generation has its own resounding clichés, but one that every generation seems to agree on is that it's ex post facto good to be original," he said. "But why? Lunatics are original. They're original all their lives."

He might as well have rammed me with a swift red car. My mind seized up. Then I became aware of Cheever's voice. "Idiocy is an unlikely subject, Louis. It lacks a certain universality."

My shoulders relaxed, and I could feel an easing of tension in the audience.

"Of course, everyone pursues the mysteries of love and death," Cheever went on. "Perhaps originality isn't the word. What one is involved in is arousal. Literature is basically a heresy. It is very much in the nature of a discovery, of bringing totally unrelated experiences into focus with one another and throwing some light on yourself. Furthermore, there is a word that's used in universities: verisimilitude. One has to give the reader a sense of truthfulness. Say you put the reader on a carpet. He's got to absolutely believe in the authenticity of that carpet before you can—and you will—pull it out from beneath him."

The word "universities" initiated a debate among the panelists about whether writing can be taught. "Why the hell can't it?" Huddle said. "Is it possible to teach somebody to play tennis? Yes, of course it is. If somebody has an athletic ability, you can teach them to play. Can you teach somebody to play the piano? Yes, the answer is yes. You can't make somebody be *gifted* at writing if they're not. If they are, there are things you can do to help them."

"What's the point of teaching someone who isn't gifted?" Simpson asked. "Is it just a commercial proposition?"

"No, I don't think so," Marsh Terry answered. "A person may take a fiction writing workshop and become a better reader."

Simpson said, "I've heard that argument before, and it seems to me like saying that the way to learn to fly an airplane is to drive a truck."

"Louis, you know, I'd hate to be piloted in an airplane by someone who couldn't drive a truck," Marsh said.

"I taught for a couple of years at Sing-Sing and the students there were *not* gifted," Cheever offered. "There were two thousand inmates, and only a few of them had the ability to put a sentence together. When I told the warden I wanted to teach a writing workshop, he said, 'Get out.' I said, 'If you don't let me in, I'm going to make trouble,' and we announced over the prison radio that we would have a class. I had decided to call it Advanced Composition. This was nine years ago. Thirty-five people signed up. It turned out that a lot of former gang members signed up, and I had to explain that this would not be a militant literature course or a power contest. One day, a student asked if he could be recognized and I said yes. He said, 'Oh what a cool motherfucker was that Machiavelli.' Seven of the men I taught have been released since then."

That symposium, that afternoon of my terror and awe, was nearly forty years ago. Now, when a student in one of my classes complains to me, as someone does each year, "It's impossible to be original. Everything's been done," I think of the week I spent in John Cheever's presence, watching him, trying to learn from him a writer's moves, a writer's way of being in the world.

In 1979 I knew nothing of Cheever's struggles with alcohol and sexuality, or the uneasy truces he'd formed with his children and his wife, but the grace of his speech and behavior, his elfin humor, seemed to answer certain questions I'd been asking myself. How does one continue to write when the money gets thin? How does one continue to craft sentences while caught in the vicissitudes of friendships, jobs, love affairs, family lives, and deaths?

Cheever provided no direct answers, but I can't overstate the importance, for me, of seeing him that week, day to day. For it's in the day to day, in each of our lives, that these questions get worked on, if not worked out. That's what I was grateful to learn one sunny week in Texas in 1979.

After the symposium, all but a few hangers-on seeking autographs left the auditorium. Cheever sat at the foot of the dais, signing books. I stood at the back of the hall waiting to take him to his hotel. When the last person had gone, and I approached him, he looked at me with sadness, wonder, and exhaustion on his face. "Tracy, are you still here?" he said.

Where the sadness and wonder came from, I don't know. Amazement, perhaps, at his recent celebrity. Melancholy over how quickly a room can empty, fame or no fame. The exhaustion was easier to account for, but it was mitigated, somewhere beneath those high, knobby cheeks, by a determination, an almost indomitable perseverance that served as his final lesson that week: the need each of us has, from time to time, whether we're writers or not, to ask ourselves, with doggedness and a bit of surprise, "Are you still here?"

Of course, these days, that question is frequently asked of literature itself. In the volcanic landscapes of the Internet, virtual reality, smart phones, and other interactive technologies, how are our notions of novel, poem, and short story changing?

In the spirit of renewal, each of us must occasionally widen our gaze, take in the whole horizon of our pursuit to examine, in all honesty, what it has meant, and why, and what it still might have to offer—to us, as well as to students and others who hope to follow our paths.

So: what *has* American literature been, what has it meant? Where were we, and where are we going?

In a book called *Harvests of Change: American Literature 1865–1914*, Jay Martin notes that the modern American novel developed as the United States, for the first time in its history, began transporting people and goods on a vast scale. After the Civil War, thousands of decommissioned soldiers canvassed the country selling paperback books. European novels were extremely popular with the new American middle class. Until the first copyright laws in 1891, U.S. publishers didn't have to pay foreign authors for their work. Dickens, Carlyle, and Thackeray swelled the salesmen's packs.

William Dean Howells and Henry James came to fiction, in part, through travel writing; Stephen Crane traveled extensively; and Mark Twain went innocently abroad.

In the twentieth century the American novel took a meditative turn. Gertrude Stein, Sherwood Anderson, Ernest Hemingway, William Faulkner, Willa Cather, and other authors writing just after the First World War raised serious doubts about the efficacy and ethics of words. Their novels are not, as Hugh Kenner says, climactic masterworks the way James's were. They are attempts to reshape the American vocabulary in the aftermath of war and the resulting loss of innocence. Picture Hemingway at dusk in scuffed boots and khakis, kicking "honor" and "glory"—concepts as tattered as blown-apart gas masks—around a steaming field of wounded men, the homeless, and the dead.

This is the literary legacy *my* teachers inherited from their teachers, and passed on to my peers and me.

In the 1960s and 1970s—the period when people my age, in love with literature, first thought seriously of becoming writers—many American novelists, shaken by the misuse of language in service to a disastrous war or to corrupt domestic politics, felt an even greater urgency to refashion American idioms. The language of the daily newspapers filled them with "wonder and awe," Philip Roth wrote in a famous essay, "also with sickness and despair," he said. "The fixes, the scandals, the insanity, the idiocy, the piety, the lies, the noise . . ." Roth trails off: words cannot convey the depth of his dismay.

He and his contemporaries had been educated by the ironic stances of novelists who had emerged, rueful and traumatized, from the Second World War: Norman Mailer, J. D. Salinger, Joseph Heller. "Catch-22" became *the* buzzword for ruinous, unsafe language. Much of the literary fiction published in the United States during the 1960s and 1970s—books by Roth, Thomas Pynchon, Susan Sontag, Ishmael Reed, William Gaddis, Joan Didion, and Donald Barthelme—was, broadly speaking, as concerned with its own fictional processes as it was in the shattering, post-atomic world, as if by dissecting itself and examining its wounds, it could purge itself of linguistic contamination.

All of this turmoil—reflected in the university curricula to which my generation was exposed—occurred against a larger philosophical debate about the nature of truth, and of literature's ability to expose the truth. I recall that Immanuel Kant was a popular figure in the philosophy and literature classes I took. In the eighteenth century, Kant said the world and its truths *are* largely fictions, a notion appearing to find support in ancient atlases, journals, and maps, long before the Americas were a sunny gleam in a sailor's eye.

For example, Gerald of Wales, reporting in 1183 on the history and topography of Ireland, wrote "There is a lake in the north of Munster which contains two islands, one rather large and the other rather small ... No woman or animal of the female sex could ever enter the larger island without dying immediately. This has been proved many times by instances of dogs and cats and other animals of the female sex. When brought there . . . they immediately died." Gerald also mentions an island where unburied human corpses never putrefy, where half-men, half-oxen and bearded women roam the fields. His account claims to be factual and was considered sacrosanct by his contemporaries.

As children of the 1960s, we didn't find Gerald's absurdities, or Kant's assertions, terribly startling. After all, we had grown up with television news broadcasts whose staged interviews and variety-show formats manipulated details with subtle skill and shaped life's mulch-pile into one obvious fiction after another. It was in twentieth century America that Kant's view of the world as a fiction may have received its strongest vindication, though perhaps not in the way he intended.

These days, we're all too aware that the fictionalization—or, in current parlance, the virtualization—of reality has quickened beyond most people's ability to reckon with it. The nature of truth has become even more elusive. And what of literature's ability to *expose* the truth?

Whatever we may think, individually, of the explosion of interactive media, one of its clear positive general consequences has been widened exposure to a greater variety of voices, a development that has touched every aspect of U.S. culture, including literature. Challenged, in part, by new media, publishers have created or sensed diverse new marketing trends based on shifting populations. Simultaneously, creative writing programs, housed on university campuses sensitive to diversity issues, are encouraging a broader range of talents than ever before. As a result, U.S. fiction is finally beginning to reflect the mix of blood, belief, and outlook that has blessed this nation—but not so many of its books—from the first.

Yet in the midst of this cultural shift, this renewal of American idioms, we hear warnings that our diversity may become so fragmented, so diffuse, eventually we'll lose our core (whatever *that* may be). We'll fly apart, leaving nothing but a hollow center.

Such fears are not new. In the fourteenth century, in *his* country, Dante sought to discover beneath the numerous dialects he heard in exile the true national language, which seemed to him near but elusive, he said, like a "panther whose fragrance hovers everywhere, tantalizing beyond entrapment."

A look back at first principles tells us that literature's core is, simply, words—a truth so obvious we tend to overlook it. As William Gass says, "[Novels and the] places and the people in them are merely made of words as chairs are made of smoothed sticks."

However varied American idioms, styles, and dialects become, however wide a net our national community casts, the individual writer is tasked, day to day, with what Philip Roth refers to as making sentences and turning them around, again and again and again, until their power is irresistible. This is a tedious process, and frequently, in the midst of it, the writer's need for renewal grows acute. Paradoxically, visits to the past, to first principles, usually *do* spark a renewal and help us map the next steps forward, sentence by careful sentence.

Briefly, then, let's slip back in time and consider a sentence by that old American travel writer Henry James. This is from *The Golden Bowl*:

> She continued to walk and continued to pause; she stopped afresh for the look into the smoking-room, and by this time—it was as if the recognition itself arrested her—she saw as in a picture, with the temptation she had fled from quite extinct, why it was she had been able to give herself from the first so little to the vulgar heat of her wrong.

The power of this sentence *is* the sentence, regardless of what the story may be about or who the character is. How does the sentence work?

To begin with, notice the word "continued"—the way its repetition creates a nervous, claustrophobic rhythm in sync with the woman's pacing. Following that, the sentence stills itself with a parenthetical aside (becoming more abstract) at the very moment the woman's attention is riveted by her glance into the smoking-room. The wording gathers force, pushed by breathy, sighing sounds—"with," "why," "give"—as the woman's realization grows, and ends abruptly on growling *r* sounds at the source of her agitation, her "wrong."

James did not distrust language as much as his literary descendants tend to do. Still, he was keenly aware of its contingencies, its gifts of prestidigitation, its power to shape the world the way a potter wets, spins, and slims a lump of clay. Characters in *The Golden Bowl* study one another, the way the reader studies James's words, for the complications of consciousness and the patterns they form. Each consciousness delineates existence for itself, and *that*, as any American novelist of any era will tell you, is a hard road to navigate. It's the heart of every trip fiction takes.

What language shows us and what remains beyond its reach; how much we can trust it: these are the shifting boundaries that make us all, on the road or locked inside our heads, perpetual refugees, perpetual immigrants in the world of words.

In the essays that follow, I will consider an individual's relationship to words by exploring, first, the nature of artistic vision and the creative person's relationship to the world; I will then turn to the practice of imagination; in the book's final section, I will focus on particular writers to try to discover how they apply their imaginations to the objects of the world. Along the way, we will be reminded of Kant, of how fictionalized our knowledge of the world has always been; of James, of the movement and pausing in his paragraphs that circumscribe accidental stumblings into meaning. And we may just discover that restlessness, perpetual movement, and accidental stumblings are further aspects of our commonality, our Americanness, to which our literature gives voice.

PART ONE

# The Literary Imagination

# Old Haunts

*America and Its Fictions*

The house of fiction has many windows
HENRY JAMES

Nature is a Haunted House—but Art—a House
that tries to be haunted.
EMILY DICKINSON

**1.**

On January 6, 2000, Michael Sager, a property manager in Tulsa, Oklahoma, was checking buildings downtown in anticipation of a cold snap. He wanted to make sure the pipes weren't leaking—that they were properly protected in case of a freeze. In particular, he was concerned about a building that had once housed an upscale restaurant, Finales, on East First Street. The restaurant had been closed for a week and the building was sitting empty, unsupervised. In an alley beside the property, by the former restaurant's kitchen door, Sager noticed liquid pooling and spilling down the street. It was peculiarly thick and crimson in color. He assumed a pipe had broken somewhere and the red-brick pavement, as well as the late afternoon light, had created the strange hue. Following the stream to its source, he saw it seeping from underneath the doors of the Francisco Ray Embalming Service directly behind the old restaurant. The blood—for that's what it was, he understood clearly now—was filling potholes in the alley three to four inches deep, and rushing to a storm sewer on the southeast corner of Detroit and First Streets, which drained into the Arkansas River. Immediately, Sager contacted the Tulsa City-County Health Department, and an inspection by a storm water management team found the blood flowing from a sewage backup in the mortuary. Subsequent investigations determined it was legal for embalmers to dispose of blood and other bodily wastes in the municipal sewer system, although the usual practice was to pack biomedical hazards in secure containers and haul them off to incinerators.

The mortuary owner was ordered to disinfect the alley using an extra heavy solution of 20 percent bleach and 80 percent water. Straight bleach was poured into the potholes and then vacuumed up. "We had lots of jokes about [the mortuary] when we opened," Patrick Hobbs, Finales's owner, told a *Tulsa World* reporter. "'If you don't like this grand finale [to your meal], we'd say, you can get the ultimate finale next door.'"

A novelist might use this anecdote and its unsettling details to convey the grittiness of urban life. I can imagine it nestling effectively inside a hard-boiled crime story, the fetid backdrop to the detective-hero's unsavory profession. But I can also imagine another context in which the gruesome imagery transcends the disgusting and causes a reader moral as well as physical queasiness, using a touch of magic (blood as living entity, moving with determined purpose): Gabriel García Márquez, say, instead of Raymond Chandler.

I discovered this bloody alley one day in a pair of newspaper articles while researching the Tulsa Race Riot Commission, a nine-member panel charged by the Oklahoma House of Representatives with conducting a historical study and developing a record of the May 31, 1921, riot in downtown Tulsa in which thirty-five square blocks were destroyed and scores of African Americans killed.

The commission had been established in 1997, eight decades after the riot; by early 2000 it was ready to issue its preliminary report. The panelists concluded that "government at all levels" had failed to provide the "moral and ethical responsibility of fostering a sense of community" that could bridge "divides of ethnicity and race" in Tulsa in the early 1920s. As a result, racial hatred was "institutionalized" in the city, "tolerated by official federal, state, county, and city policy." Therefore, on the morning of May 31, 1921, armed vigilantes provoked by the false rumor of a white woman's rape by a black man felt free to enter the African American neighborhood of Greenwood, pull families from their homes, burn the properties, murder an unknown number of people—probably hundreds—and bury them later in mass graves. To date, the Tulsa riot remains the worst occasion of racial violence in American history.

The commission recommended restitution "in real and tangible form" to survivors of the riot, most of whom were children at the time and in the late 1990s were in their eighties and nineties. Restitution "would be good public policy and do much to repair the emotional as well as physical scars of this most terrible incident in our shared past," the panelists wrote. They suggested individual compensation, as well as educational scholarships for the city's African American community.

Right away, many of Oklahoma's leaders tried to discredit restitution. "People are going to say, 'If we do this for Tulsa, where does it stop?'" said Robert Milacek, a Republican House member from Enid. "What about the Mennonites whose homes were burned during World War I? And the American Indians. We could go on forever."

Abe Deutschendorf, a Democrat from Lawton, agreed. "Who's at fault [for tolerating racial tension]? What I'm hearing is the state. Sorry . . . you did not make that argument convincing to me," he said, despite the panel's photos of several lynchings from the time, carried out with full knowledge of public officials; a Tulsa high school yearbook featuring a page of black-hooded, Klan-style "knights"; and a popular postcard from the era, sold statewide in drugstores, of a black man's torching death in southeastern Oklahoma, captioned "Coon Cookin."

My interest in the riot commission stemmed from my grandfather's long career as an Oklahoma politician and a proponent of civil rights in his state. His beliefs provided my context for the fouled alley. Here is how I saw it: thirty-five blocks of downtown Tulsa had once vanished in hateful violence. Bodies lay unclaimed—in fact, unknown—in the ground there. Now, a few folks were trying to restore the city's memory of the events, and in some small way rectify the tragedy. Powerful people, backed by money and media access, were working hard to silence them. In the middle of all this, a building started to bleed.

Editors and teachers often tell young writers, "Find your voice," but I have always been interested in the kind of literary sensibility that is drawn to the past, to voices dead and gone yet still reverberating in our lives. I am not thinking about ghost stories exactly, though from near its beginnings, in the work of Hawthorne, Poe, and others, our national literature has often dwelled in haunted houses. I am thinking about stories layered with time's multiple details—additions and the evidence of subtractions—the way old buildings, over decades, carry the scars and glories of their remodelings, revealing the history of a place.

Stories, like buildings, are social sites and mediating spaces, meeting spots for writers and their readers, carefully constructed areas where private and public lives overlap. Entering an old building, we may hear creaks and mysterious settlings—ghostly voices—speaking to us from underneath the smooth façade; may feel invisible others observing our most intimate acts. Similarly, we may wonder about the relationship between a story's surface and its foundation: how do history and memory shape, support, or warp a narrative?

I want to try to talk about the past here, its continuing presence in the deep structures of things, to see if we can learn anything, as people who inhabit both buildings and stories, from our time-haunted communal rooms with their layerings and erasures—for it has seemed to me lately that American fiction, like America itself, is increasingly faceless and present tense. As a result, it has lost much of its former substance. As the literary critic Sven Birkerts observed, "Whatever happened to the American past? Which is to say: Whatever happened to America? . . . [We have] shifted from a simple, direct, unmediated sense of reality to one that is completely mediated [by television and the Internet]. For the real we are substituting the virtual."

Community is difficult to maintain without a firm sense of history and place—and without community, who or what will foster the "moral and ethical" responsibilities that can help us overcome our social divides? Who can tell our stories accurately? The trappings of place—alleys, street grids, architecture, graffiti, stains, tire-worn grooves—as well as yesterday's failures and achievements should make us keenly aware that our biological, social, legal, and even our spiritual needs are inseparable from one another, intertwined with others, the way plumbing, wiring, and insulation come together to form public and private shelters.

2.

Various ways of addressing time and place, with varying degrees of success, have presented themselves in American literature. In *The Jungle*, Upton Sinclair's 1906 exposé of the unsanitary and exploitive conditions in Chicago's meatpacking industry, Sinclair detailed what he called the "hog squeal of the universe," the carnage of turning "eight to ten million living creatures . . . into food every year." He described a "very river of death," factory floors "half an inch deep with blood, in spite of the best efforts of men who kept shoveling it through holes." Readers of the day were so horrified by the novel's imagery, the U.S. Congress was moved to establish the Pure Food and Drug Act. But despite its profound and immediate social impact, the novel seemed to disappoint its creator. "I aimed at the public's heart and by accident I hit it in the stomach," he lamented. Sinclair was an exquisite muckraker, a troublemaker of the first rank, so it's no surprise that his prose had a visceral emotional effect. For *his* bloody buildings to touch the public's heart he needed the temperament of an elegist rather than a crusader—and here is where spending a night or two in the haunted houses of early American literature might be instructive.

In the preface to *The House of Seven Gables*, published in 1851, Nathaniel Hawthorne writes of his desire to "connect a bygone time"—its "legendary mists"—with the "very present that is flitting away from us." He distinguishes between novelists who "aim at a very minute fidelity, not merely to the possible, but to the probable and ordinary course of man's experience" and writers of romance who "manage [their] atmospheri-cal medium [so] as to bring out or mellow the lights and deepen and enrich the shadows of the picture." He respects the crusading impulses of certain writers and "would feel it a singular gratification," he says, if his work could "convince mankind—or, indeed, any one man—of the folly of tumbling down an avalanche of ill-gotten gold, or real estate," but concludes that when stories teach anything, it is "usually through a far more subtile [*sic*] process than the ostensible one." Therefore, he consid-ers it "hardly worth his while to impale [any] story with its moral . . . [as though] sticking a pin through a butterfly,—thus at once depriving it of life, and causing it to stiffen in an ungainly and unnatural attitude."

Yet, though Hawthorne refuses obvious moralizing and "minute fidelity" to things, he insists that the most crucial subject for stories is social injustice. He shares the contemporary hard-boiled novelist's disgust with our fallen world and Upton Sinclair's repugnance at human cruelty. The "wrong-doing of one generation lives into the successive ones," Hawthorne insists, until it becomes a "pure and uncontrollable mischief"—enough, perhaps, to make a building bleed. But his sense of "wrong-doing" as being timeless, or more accurately *time-haunting*, distinguishes his sensibility from that of the crusader. Had he tackled Sinclair's subject in *The Jungle*, or come across the seething mortuary in the Tulsa newspaper, he would not merely have described what he calls, in his preface, "local manners," or meddled with the "characteristics of a [specific] community." Rather, defining *place* more broadly, he would have "laid out a street that infringe[d] upon nobody's private rights . . . appropriat[ed] a lot of land which had no visible owner, and [built] a house of materials long in use for constructing castles in the air."

The Pyncheon estate in *The House of Seven Gables* is not meant to be a fantasy; Hawthorne spends considerable effort convincing us of the building's solidity. "Its whole visible exterior was ornamented with quaint figures . . . drawn or stamped in the glittering plaster, composed of lime, pebbles, and bits of glass, with which the woodwork of the walls was overspread," he writes. "On every side the seven gables pointed sharply towards the sky, and presented the aspect of a whole sisterhood of edifices, breathing through the spiracles of one great chimney. The many lattices, with their small, diamond-shaped panes, admitted the sunlight into hall and chamber, while . . . the second story, projecting far over the base . . . threw a shadowy and thoughtful gloom into the lower rooms." But this *is* a haunted house, cursed by the wrongdoing of an earlier generation, which, in its stalwart Puritanism, had persecuted and killed the land's original occupant, a man accused of witchcraft. Hawthorne's genius is not to call directly for restitution—*that* is the business of public committees—but to suggest we will all pay, those of us in succeeding generations of the American community, if we ignore or gloss over the past's mistakes. His is not a refusal of the crusading spirit, but a complex qualification of it, recognizing the persistence of both failure and possibility in human affairs. The Pyncheon house bleeds in its own manner, the "wretchedness" of history's wrongs "darken[ing] the freshly plastered walls . . . infect[ing] them early with the scent of an old and melancholy house." The mansion not only bears the traces of "outward storm and sunshine"—note Hawthorne's minute fidelity to the world, there—but also is expressive of "the long lapse of mortal life, and accompanying vicissitudes that have passed within."

A few years before Hawthorne published his novel, Edgar Allan Poe erected one of the most famous haunted houses in American literature. Though Roderick Usher's dead (or living-dead) sister, with "blood upon her white robes," is the home's ostensible ghost, the place is more generally burdened by the "ages," which have "discolored" its walls. The story is usually read as an allegory of mental collapse (the house resembles a human face with "vacant eye-like windows"), ending in the structure's "mighty walls rushing asunder," but Poe emphasizes that the vault in which the sister's body lies was once used "for the worst purposes of a donjon-keep, and, in later days, as a place of deposit for powder, or some other highly combustible substance." As in Hawthorne, there is just enough fidelity to the world here to authenticate the story's surface: the quick reference to combustible substances prepares us, somewhat, for the otherwise inexplicable ending, when the house mysteriously fragments and tumbles apart. More to the point, the past's injustices, including the tortures of a dungeon, have literally seeped into the walls and foundations of the place, eroding it with spiritual decay.

Poe writes of the Usher family's "very trifling and very temporary variation" from one generation to the next, an "undeviating transmission, from sire to son." Like Hawthorne, then (whose work he praised), Poe sees the acceptance of the past's "worst purposes" as ultimately self-destructive. The lesson, should we choose to pin it up for obvious display, is clear: left alone, old wounds will never properly heal, and will eventually break back through. The sense of grievance as time-haunting —the elegiac impulse—is what lifts these writers' materials out of the merely gruesome and Gothic, out of the didactic, and into a subtly moral realm. They hit our hearts, and the edifices of their fictions remain timeless.

Architects speak of "overdetermined" buildings, made rigidly to serve a specific purpose—a Laundromat, say. These places are doomed to destruction by their inflexibility. When the economy shifts, or the community's priorities change, and a Laundromat is no longer needed in that spot, the building must adapt to a different use—as a tax firm or a flower shop—or be torn down. In 1896 Louis Sullivan, a Chicago high-rise designer and one of the founding fathers of architectural modernism, said, "Form ever follows function," a variation of the advice young writers often receive from editors: "Form equals content." But architecturally speaking, this is unsound reasoning. Inevitably, time works changes in a place; people come and go, businesses wax and wane, styles alter, technologies shift. Most likely, a building constructed today as one kind of dwelling will, if it is to survive at all, need to serve as a different kind of establishment later on, and it is difficult if not impossible to anticipate a structure's future functions. Writers like Hawthorne and Poe seem to have borne something similar in mind in rejecting "minute fidelity" to the particulars of time and setting, and constructing instead "castles in the air." This is not to say their fiction lacks vivid detail—as we've seen, the House of Seven Gables is designed to be convincing enough to bruise your knee if you bump it—but their work, in its explicit foregrounding of past-as-ever-present, is built to house many successive generations of readers, with their various needs, desires, and views of the world.

Upton Sinclair, the tireless crusader, followed an entirely different blueprint. He targeted a specific set of conditions in a specific industry in a particular place at a precise moment in our country's development. In these ways, *The Jungle* is overdetermined. The novel still has the power to shock, and it remains a valuable historical document. We could even argue that things haven't changed much in the meatpacking world. Not long ago, the federal government charged the Hudson Foods Plant in Columbus, Nebraska, with covering up unsanitary work practices; following this announcement, the amount of meat recalled, nationwide, due to possible E. coli contamination jumped from twenty thousand to twenty-five million pounds.

Granting all this, Sinclair's achievement, impressive and important as it is, will remain at the level of the stomach, and not the heart, precisely because of its detailed attachment to a certain moment. It is time-bound, not time-haunted. Sinclair seeks an immediate social remedy—giving workers access to the means of production—without acknowledging that the remedy, like the means themselves, and the goods being produced, is never enough to satisfy timeless human cravings, loneliness, lust, the fear of death. His buildings reek with the blood of injustice, but not with the mortal decay underlying bad corporate policy.

"Finger-pointing fiction . . . addresses itself to the humanity of the dragon in the very process of depicting him as a fire-snorting monster," writes Albert Murray. "'Shame on you, Sir Dragon,' it says . . . 'be a nice man and a good citizen.' (Or is it, 'Have mercy, Massa'?)"

Perhaps we can—and we certainly should—clean the walls and change the laws whenever we see an opportunity. Sinclair is inspiring on this point. But escaping ageless human hatreds, old and ever-present perfidy, is another matter.

At bottom, most crusaders are utopians. An elegist, though possibly hopeful, possibly a social activist, knows we'll always be haunted. In the short term, writers like Sinclair may produce more measurable reform than the elegists, but by illuminating humanity's darker tendencies and their long-term consequences, the elegists have an indirect yet more powerful effect on society. "Why is it that so few moral outcry protesters . . . seem to realize . . . that all political establishments are always likely to have built-in devices to counteract the guilt and bad conscience which the exercise of power of its very nature entails?" Murray asks. "Aren't political establishments . . . likely to function much the same as some U.S. business establishments that have special departments to handle complaints, while the other transactions flow on as usual?"

The elegist accepts the dragon's bad faith—as well as his own ongoing weaknesses—and responds with imagination and creativity. An elegiac temperament doesn't produce fatalism so much as what Murray calls a "social conscience" consistent with "the actual complexity of human nature."

In this spirit, the House of Usher and the House of Seven Gables are dwellings readers can return to time and time again because *time-again* is built into their very cores, as it is into Edith Wharton's House of Mirth, or in the many-windowed fictions of Henry James (who compared Hawthorne's craft to the meticulous work of a silversmith), or in Faulkner's dusty rooms, or William Goyen's *The House of Breath*. A novel like *The Jungle* informs, entertains, even transports, but it doesn't, I suggest, offer transcendent truths beyond its immediate moments.

In our own day we have seen a number of overdetermined novels, perhaps none more notorious than Bret Easton Ellis's *American Psycho*. The novel's first publisher canceled it, fearing it captured *too* viscerally our nation's moral drift. The book effectively evoked the spirit of selfishness and greed characterizing much of the 1980s, but (despite an updated Broadway adaption in 2016) it offered no glimpse of the "wrongdoing" spirit that preceded, and made possible, that decade— and that will linger into the future. *American Psycho* will forever be a 1980s book, just as *The Jungle* will always belong to the early twentieth century. On the other hand, as one of Grace Paley's narrators says of *The House of Mirth*, recognizing its time-obsession, it's "about how life in the United States in New York changed in twenty-seven years fifty years ago" and is "more apropos now than ever."

A friend of mine who teaches American literature once admitted to me that, whenever he assigns *The Scarlet Letter*, he tells students to skip "The Custom House," Hawthorne's introduction to the novel, because, aside from its autobiographical interest, it has nothing to do with the rest of the book. This is not strictly true. The autobiographical elements are clearly embellished, and in that regard they establish the novel's narrative authority—the introduction is as much romance as the story it precedes. But at first glance the details *don't* seem essential. Hawthorne rambles for pages, complaining about a job he once held as customs officer in his old hometown of Salem, Massachusetts, a job that dulled his mind and kept him from writing. The custom house sat among "decayed wooden warehouses" where a "bustling wharf" used to thrive, he says; the "track of many languid years [was] seen in a border of unthrifty grass" behind the storehouses, where the tide overflowed. Hawthorne spent his days in a "spacious edifice of brick," far from "Paradise," beneath the drooping banner of the republic. In a cobwebbed, unfinished back room beneath dusky wooden beams, he combed daily through forgotten bundles of official documents, "materials of local history."

"It was sorrowful to think how many days and weeks and months and years of toil had been wasted on these musty papers, which were now only an encumbrance on earth," he says. But one day he claims to have discovered in the "deserted chamber" the story of Hester Prynne, written out by a former surveyor of his Majesty's Customs, as well as a "rag of scarlet cloth . . . the capital letter A." The rest, he would have us believe, is literary history, though his personal notebooks, detailing the novel's actual gestation, reveal the whole episode to be literary myth.

What is fascinating about "The Custom House" is not so much the alleged inspiration for the novel, but the elegiac atmosphere Hawthorne believed necessary for writing. In his myth, Hester's story comes to him—bleeds up, we might say, through piles of yellowed papers—in a kind of haunted house, at a time in his life when he had regained, as he puts it, a "sort of home-feeling with the past," a feeling that "haunts" him, born from his awareness that generations of his family have "mingled their earthly substance with the soil" here. Fatigued as he is by his job, he is keenly sensitive to the "sensuous sympathy of dust for dust" he perceives all around him. It is this sympathy combined with the custom house's surface of "long disuse" that puts Hawthorne in a receptive frame of mind, allowing him to properly value Hester's life. His conviction that humankind is cursed by its frailties from one generation to the next lifts his tale out of mere rage at social hypocrisy and into timeless sadness.

Significantly, the custom house is both a public building and a near-empty, deeply private place: a marriage of intimacy and social traffic, in many ways the subject of Hawthorne's novel, of all novels, and a source of endless human tension. An "enormous specimen of the American eagle with outspread wings" hung above the structure's front door, Hawthorne writes, establishing *America* as the haunted house, in dire need of exorcism.

If it is the job of public committees to conduct our national exorcisms, our investigations into possible reparations, the novelist's part in the process is to restore our memory of (sometimes deliberately) forgotten events, the unmarked graves in back of our house—not to foster fatalism, which discourages even *attempting* moral reform, but to study, in Albert Murray's words, the "whole range of human motivation," to look for the "possibility of . . . [long-term] deliverance" necessitated by social ills.

At the end of his account, Hawthorne wonders if any "great-grandchildren of the present race" will remember that a "scribbler of bygone days" once worked in this humble spot. Already, to borrow Samuel Beckett's phrase, he is joining his voice to the long sonata of the dead.

### 3.

"New ideas must come from old buildings," says Jane Jacobs, a contemporary theorist of cities. There is an echo of Hawthorne here, as if, passing by a row of decayed wooden warehouses one day, she had heard his voice saying, "How much of old material goes to make up the freshest novelty of human life." Jacobs says chain stores, chain restaurants, banks—businesses that are well established, high-turnover, standardized, or highly subsidized—can afford to demolish their old buildings and construct new ones whenever they need to grow or change or hide their sordid histories. But the people who supply these giants, continually refreshing our culture, can only afford to squat in older structures, adapting formerly abandoned spaces to their needs, storing their stuff there: books, clothing, art and industrial supplies, packaged foods, machinery parts. Jacobs calls these squatters "unformalized feeders."

One imagines Hawthorne among them, leafing happily through raw materials in the back rooms of the custom house, plucking new ideas from the dust. When I think of him there, I remember my grandfather leading me, as a kid, through the green and gold chambers of Oklahoma's House of Representatives, where he served in the late 1950s and early 1960s. He once showed me reams of thin, pink paper, the record of every motion he'd ever proposed as a state rep, every bill he'd ever drafted or supported. The papers were fusty, and the chamber struck my ten-year-old mind as spooky: big and dark, imposing, austere. "The will of the people gets done here," he told me, "and it's all based on stacks of old paper like this—ancient laws, tried-and-true ideas updated to fit our time."

He died in 1978, but I'm certain, from the record he left, he would have enthusiastically welcomed the House's formation of the Tulsa Race Riot Commission, and he would have embraced restitution as a means of stanching the blood of the past. The minutes of the panel's first meeting on November 14, 1997 begin, dryly, "After discussion ... [a] bill was introduced and passed creating ... an official study to determine what actually happened." This is certainly not the language of elegy, but the essential spirit is the same: honoring the past and acknowledging that we still exist—as in a venerable house—inside its consequences. An elegiac temperament need not oppose a crusading spirit; ideally, it enhances the effectiveness of social and political leaders by deepening their understanding of history and human nature.

For me, the power of language has always been bound up with buildings: the creeds, oaths, mottoes, and poems etched into stone in the official institutions my grandfather taught me to revere; the names of past legislators carved into copper plaques; democracy's yellowed documents preserved under glass in hallowed halls; the sad, simple names of the dead imprinted in the faces of war memorials.

Something about thin script and the tonnage of marbled walls, the combination of the seemingly ephemeral and the old and permanent, has always impressed on me the essentially elegiac nature of words. And I believe the languages of literature work together with our nation's official languages in this manner: literature is a stylization of our individual consciences and our most intimate thoughts; laws, as public decrees, are stylizations of our awareness of others. The panelist, charged with investigating legal abuses, observes ownership deeds. The novelist observes the bleeding building. The panelist calls for restitution to heal a public rift. The novelist tells us restitution is both necessary and yet wholly inadequate to heal our own souls—again, insisting on this to promote not fatalism, but generosity, an appreciation and forgiveness of the depths of human frailty. Both views are integral to our understanding of community, of the present and the past.

In 1996, a year after Timothy McVeigh blew up the Murrah building in downtown Oklahoma City, I sat by the chain link fence surrounding the void where the building once stood, reading scribbled poems and rain-smeared notes left by families from all over America to memorialize the dead. The Murrah attack had felt deeply personal to me, an ambush on the physical home of the values and language my grandfather had once shown me, here in this very city. As I sat there, a man who had survived the explosion, and who had been telling me his story all morning, pulled from his pocket a small gray stone. "A piece of the building," he said, and pressed it into my palm. "Keep it close when you write." I do, now: a wordless reminder that my words, to say anything at all worthwhile about America, need the heft of a sorrowful stone, the pressure of the past.

Ralph Ellison once noted that art and democracy converge "with the development of conscious, articulate citizens [reflected in] the creation of conscious, articulate characters" in fiction, particularly characters who can speak for the perennially disenfranchised as well as for the broader population. This is an elegant statement of art's relationship to social reform. And just as literature can shape our perceptions of public events, public events can change the ways we read literature. Immediately following the Murrah bombing, the national press lauded the survivors and the rescue workers as examples of a new "Okie" spirit. After this, it is difficult to read John Steinbeck's *The Grapes of Wrath* without overlaying mental pictures of injured children in the Murrah rubble upon images of Okies heading west in their jalopies. Similarly, any contemporary novel seeking to address historical events must be as mindful of yesterday as it is of sixty years ago.

In the early morning hours of May 31, 1921, just up the road from Oklahoma City in the Greenwood district of Tulsa, eight-year-old Kinney Booker ran with his six-year-old sister from their burning home, which collapsed behind them. They had been hiding in the attic, listening to rifle shots ricocheting throughout their neighborhood, overhearing intruders downstairs shouting at their father, "Nigger, do you have a gun?" then dragging him down the street. When smoke began to curl around them, the children fled on their own. Booker recalled, for the Riot Commission, that dozens of frightened families were surging randomly out of the neighborhood. Even the telephone poles were in flames. His sister gripped his hand and asked, "Kinney, is the world on fire?"

Until the commission made a concerted effort to locate and interview riot survivors, Booker's story, despite its drama and importance, had never been told; his words had not been recorded, not added to any public accounting, not even left abandoned in old papers for a curious customs agent to find. Only as the commission was beginning to publicize its work did a pair of novelists address the riot—Susan Straight in *The Gettin Place* and Jewell Parker Rhodes in *Magic City*. "I thought I knew history. But . . . the shame has been that for decades, even in schools here in Tulsa, children can grow up and not know something like this happened in their community," says Eddie Faye Gates, a retired history teacher and commission member who interviewed more than sixty children of the riot. "How can we expect them to learn from it and do better if we don't teach them?"

Many survivors told the commission their loved ones simply vanished. Otis Clark, who was eighteen when the attack began, never heard from his stepfather again after he was forced from his house. "Nobody knows what happened to him. There was no funeral, no memorial, no nothing." In fact, prior to the commission's report, there was only one serious legal investigation of the event: in 1926 a white man who owned a theater and a hotel in the black neighborhood sued the American Central Insurance Company for refusing payment on his ruined properties. The company cited a "riot exclusion clause" in the policies and won the case; at the trial, its lawyer admitted that a "few hundred to several thousand" white folks intended the "extermination of the colored people of Tulsa and the destruction of the colored settlement, homes, and buildings, by fire." For years, then, after the trial, another long hush fell. It was as Poe had written at the end of his Usher story: "There was a long tumultuous shouting sound like the voice of a thousand waters . . . [then it all] closed sullenly and silently"—only to bleed through the walls again, decades later.

The Tulsa riot still awaits a full, successful treatment in literature. In *Magic City*, Jewell Parker Rhodes provides an "imaginative rendering" of the event. "As a novelist . . . I envisioned a spiritual awakening that sustained the human spirit in a time of crisis," she writes. She fashions characters as "illustration[s] that prejudice blunts growth, literally and spiritually." As these statements suggest, the novel is schematic, overly earnest in its attempt to deliver a familiar truth. It is burdened by heavy-handed metaphors of escape (Harry Houdini is one of the characters' heroes). In her well-intentioned effort to offer a "spiritual awakening," Parker Rhodes overdetermines her novel; messages overwhelm mourning and experiences become illustrations, reducing the riot's enormity.

In *The Gettin Place*, Susan Straight also distills the riot and its impact. She uses Tulsa as a backdrop, in a frame with L.A.'s more recent racial unease, to foreground her meditation on violence in contemporary America. *The Gettin Place* traces the effects of hatred and economic hardship on three generations of a California family. The patriarch, Hosea, grew up in the Greenwood district of Tulsa, and he still remembers the tent his mother had to live in "on the ash-muddied ground where [her] house had burned" during the riot, how she had huddled beneath the damp white canvas with all the "others squatting like dirty hens." Eloquently, Straight describes the riot's lingering consequence for Hosea: it unmans him, stewing him in guilt over his inability as a boy to "build a shack of scrap wood" for his suffering mother. The riot is not the novel's focus, but it stands like a ruined house behind the story's major incidents, haunting each sentence. *The Gettin Place* doesn't fully reclaim Tulsa for us, for the city's history generally remains behind the scenes, but it is literature accurately formed by public events, allowing us, in turn, to resee those events with fresh understanding.

### 4.

In our present glut of digital and TV reruns, when the past is recycled for us twenty-four hours a day, readers like Sven Birkerts wonder if literature retains the power to resee the world, or whether such an activity has any value.

In arguing that it does, let me pause to offer one vivid example of literature's sustaining spirit. I mentioned this novel earlier—*The House of Breath*, published in 1950 by a young East Texan. William Goyen refurbished the old Hawthorne-Poe-vintage home, adding a few structural supports and modernizing the wiring to show how this durable nineteenth-century design could still reveal to us how we live.

The novel's young narrator, known only as Boy, is discharged from the army and returns to his now decayed family homestead in Charity, Texas, to hear his family's phantom voices call to him from the wind-animated shutters, from the empty cistern, from the cellar, from the creaking, leaf-strewn porch. His return has been prompted, after he's witnessed the chaos of many continents, by his sense of being "stripped of all [his] history" and thus "betrayed," an agony that comes upon him as he wanders through a hostile and nameless "public place," feeling "alone in the world with no home to go to." And though, once back in Charity, he laments his losses, it is clear the place's ruin has been partly self-inflicted, with the oppressive attitudes of older generations warping their children's identities. Goyen recognizes the persistence of the hateful American Puritanism vexing Hawthorne in his day. Since earliest adolescence, his narrator has grappled with sexual confusion and a barely suppressed homosexuality—a "hidden otherlife" first coaxed from him by the land itself as he swims one day in a river near his house as a boy, his erotic awareness "rising rising, faster, faster . . . [until it] burst and hurt." In the East Texas world of sawmills and the working poor, the boy knows to keep his urges in check, crushing his truest self until it is like a dry husk frozen beneath the "lacelike rime" gripping the house in winter. And he keeps quiet, waiting for "some speech the breath of the house" would breathe into him, "a language that would create and speak out into the world all passion and all despair."

His is the melancholy language of elegy, mindful of the world's sad history, which he first glimpsed in a map on his mother's kitchen wall. Like Poe's, Goyen's house is part allegory, built of human breath and bonelike walls, but it is also as substantial as the Seven Gables, located firmly in American social realities: for example, the nearby shacks of the poor "Riverbottom Nigras" flood every year, built as they are on worthless land (the only space available to blacks), and the Klan haunts these tangled East Texas woods. Prejudice, greed, suspicion, religious fervor: passed from one generation to the next, these forces, Goyen insists, institutionalize oppressive attitudes in our communities and within our individual psyches. They haunt all our dwellings.

In the Texas of *The House of Breath* there are no cattle drives or cowboys, no oil kings or beef-eating millionaires, no self-reliant heroes—none of the time-bound clichés by which the people of this region have often identified themselves. Instead, there is a time-haunted gathering of a family's "broken pieces," the need to remember fused with the need to go on—one of the most powerful and lasting fusions in literature. At the end, rooted once more in the soil where his family has lived and died, Boy sighs, "It seemed that the house was built of the most fragile web of breath and I had blown it—and that with my breath I could blow it all away."

### 5.

Through all the huffing and puffing, through depressions, riots, and wars, America's house still stands, and in the latter half of the twentieth century, as U.S. money and influence grew, we added several new wings worldwide. Perhaps now, early in a new century, we need more exterior views to understand who we are at this point in our history.

When Gabriel García Márquez writes of a "past whose annihilation had not taken place because it was still in a process of annihilation, consuming itself from within, ending at every moment but never ending its ending," he joins the fantastic—that is, death's continuing life—to the very real, sorrowful uprootings that have characterized our brutal era. In *One Hundred Years of Solitude*, his impoverished Latin American village empties out, its fictional citizens migrating toward the promise of Paradise, the "chimerical Negroes in the cotton fields of Louisiana, the winged horses in the bluegrass of Kentucky, the Greek lovers in the infernal sunsets of Arizona, the girl in the red sweater painting watercolors by a lake in Michigan who waved . . . with her brushes, not to say farewell but out of hope, because she did not know that she was watching a train with no return passing by." On an unprecedented planetary scale now, people scatter and break like their belongings, leaving empty homes, bones, shards, and captured breaths in bottles for later generations to wonder at.

In 1955, sixteen years before *One Hundred Years of Solitude* appeared in English, the Mexican writer Juan Rulfo published *Pedro Páramo*, a novel narrated from the tombs of a desert town called Comala, and one of the single most prescient narratives in our age of mass diasporas. García Márquez knew the book well—he said his discovery of Rulfo "showed [him] the way to continue . . . writing."

Juan Preciado, *Pedro Páramo's* initial narrator, returns to his old village to find his father but meets only blood-drained spirits, hears only voices whispering from "walls stained red by the setting sun." In time, the reader understands that Juan himself is dead; like his country, he has dried up and blown away, the victim of a greedy *cacique*, a lonely Fisher-King with the power to close his arms and smother all life. In Rulfo's world, the living, to paraphrase Nietzsche, are merely a slightly more active version of the dead. As in Hawthorne's tale of the Pyncheons, we have a ghost story here, but also much more: a crime tale in its cruelest sense. Rulfo said he modeled Comala on a real Mexican village called Tuxacuesco, which became a ghost town in the 1940s because "everyone [went] away as braceros"—that is, they migrated to the United States to serve as cheap labor in the fruit fields. Comala is haunted by poverty and unjust economics like those found in *The Jungle* and *The Grapes of Wrath*—by a needy American monster as much as by restless specters. Like Hawthorne and Poe, Rulfo joins the eerie timelessness of Romance with a keen awareness of ongoing social realities—a rueful mix of capitalism and ectoplasm—and he does so from a perspective possible to North Americans only if we leave our home from time to time and take a walk around the outside of the house.

## 6.

These days we are more likely to hear about "sick" buildings than haunted ones, indoor environments polluted by toxic presences: the pesticides, cleaners, and glues in the cabinets beneath our kitchen sinks; the herbicides and weed killers in our garages; the low-level radiation from microwaves, televisions, computer screens. Even the Washington, D.C., home of the Environmental Protection Agency, which monitors such things, suffers: recently, 10 percent of the building's workers had a severe allergic reaction to a new carpet. The EPA predicts that 4-phenylcyclohexene, a chemical compound used to make the latex backing on most carpets for the last forty years, can cause nervous system and genetic problems—but no one knows how to eliminate the chemical's production from the current manufacturing process. Furthermore, most carpets are treated with formaldehyde finishes and pesticides to mothproof them.

Still, whether we are chasing hidden ghosts or a hidden gas leak, our abiding interest must be with the way our private lives fit into a larger human community, the way our selves are restricted or aided by public pressures. And despite our current cultural fascination with the instantaneous and the virtual, old buildings and time-haunted narratives still offer the profoundest glimpses of how we have chosen to live decade after decade, and they best illuminate the consequences of our choices.

Frank Duffy, the cofounder of a prominent British design firm, once said, "A building properly conceived is several layers of longevity"—a record of human etchings and erasures, changed desires, new needs, second looks, misgivings, wrong turns, disasters and lucky scrapes, remote reasons, enormous last-minute changes. And prose narrative, that sprawling slumgullion of a form, able to house thoughts, talk, exposition, sermons, curses, and poetry, is, like an ancient structure stained and odorous with years of human use, a natural repository of our leavings.

Nowadays, gauging the degree of our cultural sickness, we might notice, as Donald Barthelme does in his novel *Paradise*, "Metal detectors set up at the entrances of schools. Gun-toting Wackenhuts in supermarkets (part of the design). Enter a jewelry store," he writes, "and above the selling floor there's a booth with bullet-proof glass with gun ports and a guy with a shotgun. Giant concrete flowerpots all around the Capitol which have nothing to do with love of flowers." Or we might paw through the mulch piles in our backyards, discovering, as a John Updike character does, a "virtual snowfall of pale plastic litter—container tops, flexible straws, milk containers . . . tinted bottles of a nostalgic thickness." In either case—the public or private glance—the interest lies in what our dear, flawed lodgings indicate to us about our paranoia and our routines, our repressed and irrepressible memories, our dreams and desires.

7.

Ezra Pound urged poets and writers to "make it new." I suppose I've been suggesting the opposite here. Albert Murray says the most "urgent necessity for any writer who truly takes the social . . . [and] ethical function of fiction seriously is not to create something new, but rather to achieve something natural to himself and to his sense of life, namely a stylization adequate to the complexity of the experience of his time and place." I would add that we must also value history, not for nostalgia's sake, but for the sake of a future *enriched* by the past.

The latest fashions, movies, music, and buildings may reveal who we think we are, or who we're striving to be, at this moment in our cultural development, but they are untested, too unfinished to tell us what we love most—what "remains American" over time, to quote the poet Richard Hugo.

Still, like filmmakers, architects, musicians, and fashion designers, writers today are under increasing cultural pressure to embrace placelessness and the cursor-marked present. Our current technological revolution and our vaunted "free global market" promote homogeneity and mass production; consumers have been trained to expect familiar imagery, instant gratification, and convenience. Sven Birkerts again: "We are . . . entrusting to software the various gathering, sorting, and linking operations that we used to perform for ourselves and that were part of the process of thinking about a subject." As a result, the "great muscle of memory" atrophies, and we lose sight of our aspirations, our best intentions.

Perhaps the old haunted house, with its bloodstains and tormented whispers, remains our most vivid reminder that the present does not exist without the past, and that even our most stunning virtual worlds will one day endure merely as rubble in mounds of other junk. As designer Stewart Brand notes, when a room "becomes not what happened in it, but what its square footage is worth," when it is "devoid of history," it becomes nobody's home.

Early in America's life, Thomas Jefferson's sense of history led him to a profound faith in place. He believed that allotting fifty acres—a stake in the land—to every American family would guarantee the moral values on which democracy depends. Long before the virtual revolution, our nation lost this faith. But, as historian Patricia Limerick reminds us, "from the caves in the lava beds of Northern California, where the Modocs held off the United States army for months, to the site along the Mystic River in Connecticut, where Puritans burned Pequots trapped in a stockade, the [North American] landscape bears witness to the violent subordination of [a people]. These haunted locations are not distant, exotic sites set apart from the turf of our normal lives." Despite the enticements of the virtual, "neither time nor space . . . can insulate us from these disturbing histories."

I'll end with the work of a writer who understood the past's presence in our lives better than almost anyone. In the tradition of Hawthorne and Poe, John Cheever turned his gaze toward private rather than public histories, but he layered time and space precisely in the ways Limerick suggests.

The narrator in Cheever's haunting story "The Seaside Houses" leases various old beach homes year after year for his family's summer vacations. At one point he remarks, "Sometimes the climate of [a particular house] seems mysterious, and remains a mystery . . . who, we wonder, is the lady in the portrait in the upstairs hallway? Whose was the Aqualung, the set of Virginia Woolf? Who hid the copy of *Fanny Hill* in the china closet, who played the zither, who slept in the cradle, and who was the woman who painted red enamel on the nails of the claw-footed bathtub? What was this moment in her life?" He recalls making love with his wife in a strange room smelling of "someone else's soap," and adds, "in the middle of the night the terrace door flies open with a crash, although there seems to be no wind, and my wife says, half asleep, 'Oh, why have they come back? Why have they come back? What have they lost?'" By the story's end, this somber meditation adds another ghost to its chambers: "This is being written in another seaside house with another wife," the narrator, a faithless husband, confesses quietly. "I sit in a chair of no discernible period or inspiration. Its cushions have a musty smell.... In the middle of the night, the porch door flies open, but my first, my gentle wife is not there to ask, 'Why have they come back? What have they lost?'"

Cheever's elegant, melancholy prose and his elegiac sense save his stories from becoming trivial listings of middle-class complaints, records of the suburban gentry's bad behavior, as his critics often claim.

At the end of "Goodbye, My Brother," he writes, "The sea that morning was iridescent and dark. My wife and her sister were swimming ... and I saw their uncovered heads, black and gold in the dark water. I saw them come out and I saw that they were naked, unshy, beautiful, and full of grace, and I watched the naked women walk out of the sea." Our throats catch on the simple phrase, "that morning," tinged with time's fleetingness. That morning is over now, and no matter how many times the narrator repeats, "I saw ... I saw ... I watched," as if to convince himself the moment really happened, he can't get his history back. He is left only with beauty's trace, like the afterglow of a Roman candle in the sky. We are left with lament.

This is very different from Bret Easton Ellis's take on privileged lives, though arguably he and Cheever write about the same class of people: "She was scared, [but] a few shots of vodka in the back of the limo along with the money I'd given her so far, over sixteen hundred dollars, relaxed her like a tranquilizer," says *American Psycho's* narrator, Patrick Bateman, after picking up a prostitute. "Her moodiness turned me on and she acted like a total sex kitten when I first handed her the cash amount—six bills attached to a Hughlans silver money clip."

Timing is everything in a sentence—and in a *sensibility*. Just as Cheever slips "that morning" into his paean to beauty, dimming the joy with sadness, Ellis slips the "Hughlans silver money clip" into his characters' tragic transaction, emphasizing his true interest: minute fidelity to *things*.

Granted, thing-love is *American Psycho's* strategy. Praising the book, Norman Mailer wrote, "When an entire new class thrives on the ability to make money out of the manipulation of money, and becomes altogether obsessed with the surface of things—that is, with luxury commodities, food, and appearance, then, in effect, says Ellis, we have entered a period of the absolute manipulation of humans by humans."

But an obsession with the surface of things is only one part of human experience. Cheever's characters dote on their vodkas and their cars and their sexual peccadilloes, but he pushes his stories so much further than the immediate moment—not always into the past, but at least into the present moment's turning, like a leaf in late summer, from *what is* to *what was*. Ellis, like Sinclair in his day, argues that our culture and our morals are decaying, and that the decline can be blamed on rampant consumerism. Cheever moves past the point of blame into the much richer, much more timeless territory of human loss and need.

In his story "The Enormous Radio," when the Westcotts—a respectable middle-class couple living in a New York apartment building—buy a new radio to go along with their other luxury items, they soon discover that listening to Mozart quintets isn't enough to deliver them from their daily disappointments. But Cheever isn't content with the easy irony of the "good life's" failures. Eventually, Irene Westcott begins receiving her neighbors' noises on the radio; through some acoustical quirk, she can listen in on the lives around her—the electric razors, the doorbells, the Waring mixers, the arguments, the laughter, the crashing dishes, the discussions of doctor bills and bank overdrafts. Her apartment is haunted with voices; for her, the building becomes a horror show of the cravings, recriminations, loss, and useless distractions on which people depend to get through their days. When all of this is mixed with the radio's regular newscasts—"An early morning railroad disaster in Tokyo," "A fire in a Catholic hospital near Buffalo"—Irene is overwhelmed, as is the reader, with much more than the glut of *things* and the broken promises of material culture; she weeps for the "restrained" and unchanging "melancholy of the [human] dialogue."

In Cheever's world, all of us stumble through ever-dimming rooms, nicked and scraped by the sharp edges of tables, desks, mirrors, and sinks that will probably outlast us. Stained with our leavings, the obsessive scratchings of our passions, they will stand as witnesses, not quite mute, to the cruel or gentle lives we have lived.

Ruefully, Cheever records that in most American cities—unlike Rulfo's Comala—the "unexalted kingdom [of the dead] is on the outskirts, rather like a dump, where they are transported furtively as knaves and scoundrels and where they lie in an atmosphere of perfect neglect." But his fiction, like Hawthorne's and Poe's, suggests that the cost of neglecting our dead is spiritual poverty and disgrace. Cheever recalls both Walter Benjamin, who said, "Death is the sanction of everything the storyteller can tell. He has borrowed his authority from death," and John Berger, who says that the finest storytellers, brimming with an awareness of time and the ever-present past, watch life "as life might watch itself."

Our sense of our surroundings *does* appear to be eroding. Old buildings topple; new ones seem more and more temporary. As I write, New York University plans to destroy a Greenwich Village house where Edgar Allan Poe once lived in order to construct a new law school building. "Nevermore," the spirits that once haunted those rooms and enriched American art. Recently, I heard an engineering professor extol the Internet's virtues, insisting that face-to-face encounters were overrated, that physical classrooms were more trouble than they were worth. It costs too much money and time, he said, to maintain *place*. He believes learning occurs more efficiently online, in the no-place, no-fixed-hours of cyberspace. Now, with moocs and the like, this vision is gaining currency in education, business, government, and will no doubt find a bigger voice in our national and international literature.

Samuel Beckett's settings will come to seem quaint next to the chic prose wastelands of the future. But real skeletons will continue to be hidden in real closets, the "worst purposes" will unfold in actual dungeons, truck bombs will shatter material buildings with mortal people inside, and tangible neighborhoods will fall in genuine flames. A storyteller who flees from ghosts, seduced by the illusions of freedom from time and place, flees the very source of storytelling; fails to learn how best to be a citizen of both the nation and of art; fails to see past the merely gruesome and into a subtly moral realm; fails to understand how, one morning, as small leaders continued to reject the cries of the past, a building started to bleed in Tulsa.

# Company

I know what George was wearing that night. Not because I remember, exactly, but because he always wore the same thing in those days: a pair of cut-off Levis, frayed white threads noodling over his knees, and a gray T-shirt stained with Jack Daniels. I also know, from his habits rather than from any particular memory, that as he told me his story he smoked one Kent after another and lined up the butts in a square gold ashtray on his desk. He had tied a blue scarf round his skull as a sweatband. He sipped his Jack from a chipped yellow glass and bobbed his head to Tom Petty as he fished up details of a New Orleans bar (sawdust on the floor, a black and white Magnavox tuned to the Saints over the racketing Foosball machines) where he'd once got into a fight over a woman he couldn't remember. She was black. That's about the best he could do.

I recall walking to George's apartment that night, on a moonless, starlit street, past a Kwik-Lube and an E-Z Mart, wondering, *When did Houston get so ugly?* I guess I was in a bad mood.

I remember he made me laugh. He always made me laugh. I remember his drinking, worse than usual, had me worried. I wish I could remember his soft, lovely voice: a poet's voice, full of music, quips and quirks.

Oh, I *do* remember it, of course, it plays in my head, but no louder than the hiss on a car radio when you've traveled too far and the oldies station *should* be on the dial but can't be located anymore.

I lost the cassette tape—and the machine, defunct technology—on which I recorded George that night. Except as down-low static, his voice is no longer available to me.

I had asked him to tell me the story of the bar fight as part of an assignment I'd received from a linguistics teacher. "Get someone you know quite well to tell you a story," the teacher had said. "Record it and transcribe it word for word. A week or so later, ask the person to type out the sequence of events." It was an exercise in comparing writing to speech. How would the accounts differ in specifics and tone? What factors—the intimacy of face-to-face, the booze, and Tom Petty, as opposed to enforced solitude, a lengthier time for reflection—would explain the differences? Beforehand, I could surmise that the written version would be tighter. Writing is self-conscious in a way that shooting the shit with a friend is not.

In any case, over the years, along with my cassette tapes, I misplaced the transcript of George's story and his written testimony. I can't tell you now the name of the bar where George took a swing at a guy. I can't say what was so fine, if anything, about the woman he fought for. What did I learn from the linguistics exercise? Hard to say. What I remember is my friend, dead now from lung cancer (all those damn cigarettes!).

No.

I don't remember him nearly well enough.

What I remember when I remember my friend is how much I miss him, his sweetness, his musical voice.

Which is to say: at this stage of my life, neither speaking nor writing is worth a damn. Talk is cheap. Writing is even cheaper (think: ad copy. *Kwik-Lube Will Get You On the Road!*). Words cannot return my friend to me. Yet the memory of his speech, and his writing (if I had not been so careless as to lose it), serve as companions for me in his absence. Good company.

So I'm wrong.

Words *are* worth something, after all.

Perhaps language's greatest pleasure is its self-negating quality, its ability to start an argument with itself, to get a dialogue going: the very essence of companionship.

Regarding argument: In *Vernacular Eloquence: What Speech Can Bring to Writing*, Peter Elbow says, "Because writing can conserve speech—speech that time wipes out—it tends to function as a conservative force—in the various senses of the word. By preserving texts, writing is usually a force for stability. And yet, paradoxically, writing can help those who *resist* tradition. It is only in a literate culture that the past's inconsistencies have to be accounted for, a process that encourages skepticism and forces history to diverge from myth."

So I argue with myself.

The myth of my friend George (not because the details are false, but because I've given them an amber glow, by now, in repeated anecdotes): his sweetness, his musical voice.

George's actual history: bar fights, too much smoking and drinking. I remember he cut short the story of the fight that night because he had a rendezvous with his upstairs neighbor, a woman with whom he was having an affair. She worked in a hospital down the street. He said he didn't know her name. He called her The Nurse.

Peter Elbow's title, *Vernacular Eloquence*, echoes the title of Dante's revolutionary book from the early fourteenth century, *De Vulgari Eloquentia*, in which Dante argued that the "vernacular spoken language of his region of Italy was 'nobler' than the Latin used for any serious writing at the time." Dante praised the "language of children and illiterate women," its directness, the intensity of its feeling, preferring it to stuffy, official texts decreeing this, that, and the other (including how people should write).

When he penned *The Divine Comedy*, Dante scored the music of Eternity to the language of nursemaids.

I remember now. I remember the name of the bar. The Rabbit Hole. The meditative state of mind induced by writing has just called forth these words. Does the name of the place make George—his past, his motives for fighting there—come any clearer?

That certain properties of speech can enliven writing is a delightful discovery. Fragments. Interjections. Sidetracks and meanders. Directness. Useful repetitions.

Elbow points out that writing often tends toward *nominalization*, that is, turning actions into entities, verbs into nouns. He offers the following example: "The conversion of hydrogen to helium in the interior of stars is the source of energy for their immense output of heat and light." Here, the *action* of the chemical transformation is a done deal, all neatly packaged in a phrase: the "conversion of hydrogen." This language has the advantage of compression, a valued quality in formal writing, but it doesn't put out much heat.

Furthermore, Elbow says, nominalization emphasizes *product* over *process*. What gets the nod here is the "source of energy" (following the only verb in the sentence: "is") as opposed to the process, front and center, in a verby, more speech-like sentence such as, "Stars convert hydrogen to helium, and that's how they get enough energy to radiate heat and light."

When we worry about compression and the like, we feel hidden eyes on us, the eyes of Tradition, of wrist-slappers wielding sharp wooden rulers. We feel the presence of power and hierarchy. Judgment.

When we speak most freely, we feel comfortable. Or: We feel comfortable, so we're able to speak more freely. Booze can help. So can Tom Petty. The presence of a friend.

These days, when I hear George's voice most clearly in my head, it's not generalized the way writing often is; I mean, I don't succeed at overlaying the memory of his voice onto any old phrase.

When I'm haunted by him now, it's in the form of something I actually *did* hear him say over and over, "Lord love a duck!" when he was happy or surprised, or "I was drunk as a skunk that night." Or I hear a memorable sentence from a very specific occasion—say, the day he called to tell me about his cancer: "Shit, I'm in trouble, man."

Elbow notes writing's tendency to move forward into left-branching, rather than right-branching structures.

Here's a left-branching sentence: "Compelling me to examine the history as well as the myths of my friend, this essay serves to clarify George to me as well as to the reader."

A right-brancher: "This essay clarifies George to me and the reader by compelling me to examine his history as well as his myths."

The leftie forces us to bear in mind the first part of the sentence, without quite knowing what it means, while we wait for the explanatory context. Speech is more likely to produce a right-branching sentence. When we talk we're typically less concerned with formality or elegance. We want to get to the point. Naturally, Elbow argues that writing can benefit from this impulse. It's good to get to the point. The child wants her supper. The nursemaid wants her bedpan. The poet wants his Heaven.

The woman's name was Jamie. I remember now. Jamie in The Rabbit Hole.

The whole point of speaking and writing is to organize experience, preserve, and remember. Yet George admitted he couldn't clearly recall Jamie, and his accounts of her differed. She was the missing center of his story, and now of this essay.

As he spoke about his bar fight, George's tone swung from cavalier to fatherly (from *Yeah, I was a bad-ass* to *Don't try this*). George was a few years older than I was and he liked to give me life-lessons. Of course, his tone loosened up as he drained the bottle of Jack, cranked up *Damn the Torpedoes* ("Break down, go ahead and give it to me!"), and the clock ticked toward his assignation with The Nurse.

All of this—the story-telling occasion—is hard to replicate on the page. On the page, tone depends on word choice, word order. Syntax. Rhythm. Sound. If I could voodoo up the verbal equivalent of rock 'n' roll, bourbon, and erotic anticipation, I'd be cooking with gas.

Elbow mentions "intonation units," measuring the amount of information a person can absorb at any moment, usually timed to an inhale or an exhale, *breath* as *sense*. Reminds me of Alfred Hitchcock's rule for movie length: a motion picture should never be longer than the human bladder's capacity for holding its piss.

The night George talked about Jamie, he voiced a particular version of himself, perhaps for his entertainment as well as mine, but also, in his fatherly mode, as a way of instructing me about the wages of drunkenness and foolish infatuation. What I remember about the spoken version of the story is a hum of embarrassment beneath a boastful scrim: *I knocked that asshole clear into the next county but then I turned to look at Jamie and Good Lord, that woman was foul, what was I thinking?*

By contrast, the written account was forgiving. Self-justifying. *Of course I got drunk. Look what that woman had done to me. But seriously, she was fine!* With only himself for company, George was gentler with the man in the mirror.

Which account was history? Myth?

And *my* role as hearer? As reader? On reflection (that is, as I write this) it seems to me now that George's drinking that night had to do with me, with the fact that I'd asked him for a story about his bad behavior and that, as an older man, a man looking out for me, he felt conflicted about that. How would he pitch his persona? If he played the fool—for laughs, for the sake of imparting bitter wisdom—would he diminish himself in my eyes? Would our friendship suffer?

Alone, George was closer to talking to himself. To what degree that admitted more honesty, only he knew.

The profoundest knowledge, says Peter Elbow, is the "linguistic knowledge that's *in the body.*" The body that speaks, whose words are lost to time. The body that forgets. And dies.

When it came time for George to meet The Nurse, he saw me to the door (following me, on his way up the wooden staircase in the hallway, with a fresh bottle of Jack in his hand). I walked back down the moonless street past the Kwik-Lube and the E-Z Mart. Above me, hydrogen was turning into helium. In the store's parking lot I noticed two medics loading a stretcher into the back of an ambulance. On it, an unconscious woman. Young. Black. From a distance, I watched a cop interrogate a drunk white boy sitting on the curb in front of the store, next to an old yellow Mustang. Its driver's side door hung open. I gathered he had pulled into the parking lot too fast and struck the woman, who was now speeding toward the hospital down the street.

It occurred to me: the hospital might page The Nurse for emergency duty. Abandoned, George could return to his apartment, give me a call, and finish his story for me.

The young man referred to his car as "the beater." "I've driven this ol' beater for years. I knew what I's doin'. Trust me, man." The cop called the Mustang "the vehicle." "Isn't it the case that you were operating the vehicle at an excessive rate of speed?" Writing-gear speech (Elbow calls it), nowhere near the young man's universe of discourse.

What could these guys possibly say to each other?

And the woman? Let's call her Jamie. I'll wager that, no matter what was said or written that night on the policeman's pad in the parking lot, neither the cop nor the driver of the beater would remember her later. Not nearly well enough.

And so, while George and The Nurse have at it (God bless you, man, have yourself a ball), and *E* and *Z* flicker mutely at the sky, let's try to stop time, to organize and preserve our thoughts. Just for a moment. A spot, as Wordsworth would have it. No speech. No scribbled testimonies.

Silence (is it possible to *write* silence?).

Here's to Jamie.

# What It Was, What It Could Have Been

As a child, Tracy Harris stared at her father's architectural drawings and wondered what kind of magical maps she was seeing. Were these skeleton-sketches, animal anatomies? Were they shellfish? When she realized she was looking at representations of buildings, she was still intrigued by her father's designs, but what they were was not as mesmerizing as what they could have been. When she was free to imagine the diagrams as many things at once, she believed she held in her hands the blueprints of the universe, clues to the ghostly codes underlying existence. When she knew they were only simple rooms made for humble objects (flowers in a pot, a cabinet full of china, a couch), they lost much of their spell. "One of the things I'd like people looking at my work to feel is the magic I experienced when I saw those drawings for the very first time," Harris says. "But of course most people don't feel what I did when they look at engineering sketches. You have to not know what they are. A confusion has to be present."

She adds that she was probably dyslexic as a child; this may have increased the world's sweet perplexity for her. She couldn't understand two-dimensional plans of elevations. "Also, I grew up in a pretty uncontrolled household," she says. "It was okay to make a mess, to build volcanoes on the dining room table out of whatever materials you could find, and leave it there for weeks." Her grandfather was also an architect; frequently, her babysitters were drafting supplies. "I could take things apart—like clocks—and no one would even notice. I didn't successfully put them back together. I tried. But I found it was interesting to dismantle something, try to reassemble it, and come up with a completely different object": a thing that never was that haunts what eventually came to be.

Tracy Harris is a painter with a literary imagination, the kind of visual artist from whom writers can learn to see the past's influence on the present. She is also aware that words, like things, often slip their anchors. Today, that elusiveness bothers her. She's trying to be accurate. We're sitting in a coffee shop in Dallas on a late fall afternoon. She grips her cup as though it might shake apart (who knows what possibilities objects possess?). She leans into a sentence, pauses, and then sinks in her chair, staring shyly at the table. Finally, as a way of explaining the difficulties she has in discussing her work, she says, "Before I even knew his ideas, I was attracted to Wittgenstein because I read that almost all the books attributed to him were written by students, from his lectures. He'd rarely publish anything himself because he could never trust his own words. Toward the end of his life he refuted everything he'd said in the *Tractatus*, his first book. And so much of what he was saying seemed just beyond his verbal grasp . . ."

The *Tractatus* concludes, "Whereof one cannot speak, thereof one must be silent." It's a monologue stippled with pauses, lost finally in a tangle of self-negations. At the end of the book, Wittgenstein claims that the truth of his thoughts is unassailable even though his ideas are "nonsensical."

Harris's paintings share this paradoxical spirit, and that's why they're hard to talk about.

Wittgenstein elevates certain kinds of nonsense to a level of great importance; by nonsense he means a grasping after metaphysical truths, of whose existence he was skeptical but deeply respectful. The layerings and erasures in Harris's paintings demonstrate a similar measure of skepticism and deference toward the unseen universe. She leaves visual records of grasping, filled with precise grids (echoes of her father's architectural designs) and nonsense (childlike scribbles). The paintings are both assertive, in the authority of their geometric marks, and silent, in their built-up surfaces, half-concealing abandoned plans. In her work, the past is ever-present, the stillborn vitally alive. She has found a way to paint ideas, and to paint everything at once, yet her work trembles with uncertainty, the shakiness of the human hand.

Her all-inclusiveness is reflected in reviews of her work. "Harris is ... attracted to the imagery of dramatic weather," says *ARTnews*. "Pale yellows, blues and greens, her colors are peaceful unless they explore the dark, mysterious turbulence of storms." One reviewer says her paintings "have the appearance of the purposeful jottings of an inspired inventor." Another says they resemble "turbines, cogs, pulleys, wheels, and even flowers," while a third compares them to "star-riven midnight skies, magical cave drawings or shimmering ocean floors."

"I'm more interested in seeing the permutations, the different paths an idea might take, than the finished product," she says. "All the different possibilities and especially the ones that wouldn't be viable."

Compulsively, she leaves "trails of decisions"—and indecision—on the surfaces of her work. Her most recent paintings are efforts at mapping life itself, recording failure as well as success, like a Natural Selection chart with lines of extinction, paths of growth.

When she was seven, Harris took art lessons from a woman who painted on china. The teacher arranged still-lifes for her students to sketch, composed of cups and vases and plates. These traditional subjects have left traces, like fossils, in Harris's work, faint exoskeletons in thick, muddy earth tones. A viewer comes upon them in the paintings the way an anthropologist discovers something long buried in the planet: a timeless image. "The cup is a universal shape for the reproductive parts of plants and animals," she explains. "It's also the form for weights and pendulums."

In her hands, a china cabinet becomes a meditation on the birds and the bees. The history of art is here along with the history of science, for these objects have long been the subject of Western painting and study. Harris's gaze sees through them: she's not after the beauty of external shapes, she's probing their deep structures, taking them apart with little hope of putting them back together again. In this way, the conventional subjects of art and the methods of science collide, charging the paintings with tremendous wit. If their angular lines and multiple images recall the Cubism of Picasso and Braque, they also resemble the obsessive sketching in Leonardo's notebooks. If the flat surfaces and broad gestures invite comparisons to Abstract Expressionism, they also remind us of the charts we've seen in Chaos Theory textbooks: lines of connection, renderings of invisible forces.

"All the disciplines—science, art, literature, religion—are connected," she says: a writerly way of looking at the world. "It's the search for the way existence is ordered." She recalls her delight in Leonardo's doodles, the way *he* mixed disciplines. She especially loved the "way he placed an obstruction in the path of water, and mapped the flow of water around it." Recording a trail of absence, a hint of the hidden laws that haunt the world. "The first time I saw that, it changed the way I felt my work build . . . the idea of tracing something that would seem to be unpredictable, and finding patterns."

When I first saw her work, more than forty years ago now, it was mostly—though not strictly—representational. "I never painted straight still-lifes," she recalls. "Even when there were recognizable literal elements—vessels of various kinds—I'd make drawings of those very same objects and put them in the paintings." In effect, she established dialogues between rough designs and their final results. "I'd also add all kinds of structures in the background that would change the space. It flattened out and tore in places."

I remember a painting she made of a friend disappearing into a couch. In the middle of a cushion, vortices appeared, as though a black hole had suddenly erupted/collapsed in an ordinary Dallas apartment, swallowing a man. "Yes, I did a whole series of those," she says. "Vanishing roommates."

In a more recent painting, *Entrances and Exits to the World*, the vortices are there but the couch is gone. She's abandoned the surface for what's hidden beneath; stripped away empirical experience to seek its underpinnings. Her concerns have remained remarkably consistent across the years, even as she has deepened her vision and expanded her pictorial vocabulary.

Talking to her, one begins to believe that, indeed, the cup in her hand could shake apart and refigure itself. A pendulum, a weight. A swirl through time.

Harris's father moved the family from Dallas to Bangkok for four years when she was in middle school. He was in the Army and Air Force Exchange, and wound up as chief architect and engineer, designing military bases.

Harris was fascinated by the shapes of the ziggurats she saw in Bangkok: giant vessels filled with prayer. Years later, when she read Dante in college, she connected the vortex-shapes of the ziggurats with the spiraling circles of the Inferno. "A far-off windmill turning its huge sails / when a thick fog begins to settle in, / or when the light of day begins to fade, / that is what I thought I saw appearing," Dante writes of his journey beneath the surface of the earth. The description could well apply to some of Harris's paintings.

A number of thinkers believe existence is ordered in "several planes, like an envelope structure," she explains. "You go through one envelope-layer, then you go on. The repetition of that structure is really interesting. Vessels, spaces, apertures . . . these images show up in so many native traditions. Among the Mayans. In the Ukraine. They really are archetypes."

"It's a spiritual experience for me to make the paintings," she adds, "though it's certainly not connected to any specific religion. I'm trying to describe something I don't have the answers to."

Like Rothko's late works, her paintings are genuine acts of faith— attempts to define the dimly perceived, to locate a properly worshipful attitude.

Drawing and architecture have remained touchstones throughout Harris's life. One summer, she took a break from her graduate studies in Dallas and followed her boyfriend to San Francisco to build an apartment. "I thought we were going there to paint a garage door. That's what my boyfriend told me. When we got there, his friends gave us the plans and left. They wanted a guest apartment in their basement. It's illegal to do that without a permit, so they couldn't hire someone there. . . . I wound up doing everything from the framing and the duct work and the wiring to pouring concrete and sheet-rocking and piercing walls to put in windows. A contractor did come by periodically to make sure we weren't blowing all the fuses. Building this place felt more real to me than what I'd been doing in school. The physicality of it was compelling."

And in a sense she was working inside one of her father's drawings from long ago.

"This was about the time I started to read a lot in physics," she says. The apartment owner was a writer, a man named Peter Delacorte, whose family used to own Dell Publishing. His personal library was stocked with Einstein and other physicists, as well as Wittgenstein and Stephen Jay Gould. The elements that would form Harris's later style were locking into place. She began to study, systematically, the similarities between fossilized trilobite skeletons and electrical charts, between the ziggurats she'd seen as a child and Einstein's diagrams of space and time.

As part of her MFA work at Southern Methodist University, she studied with Mel Bochner, a visiting artist-in-residence. Bochner first came to prominence in the 1960s as one of the American minimalists, making drawings, paintings, sculptures, installations—"an art," one critic said, "audaciously ascetic and aggressively obscure." A rigorous mathematical purity characterizes much of his work, as well as a relentlessly investigative eye. "I wanted to find a foundation for my art that I could believe in," he once said. "It meant getting rid of all the things that I didn't know from my own experience." Harris found his philosophical approach to art both congenial and inspiring. In the early 1980s, when she studied with him, he was making oil paintings that collapsed figure and ground, challenged the architecture of the room in which they were displayed through masses of color, arcs, and planes that seemed to pull away from the wall. He had also just completed a series of drawings called *Skeletons* in which pentimenti of colors and lines wrestled each other in a tangle of order and fury.

"I think there are two parts to painting," he has said. "There are the things you can control, and the things you can't. You hope that the things you can control . . . the knowledge that you have . . . the background of experience, is built up to the point you can trust it. And something surprising comes from this trust when you confront it with the things you can't control."

Confrontation and lack of mastery became Harris's strategies as she completed her graduate degree. "By the time I got back from San Francisco, I was trying to eliminate all elements of decorativeness from my work," she says. "I felt uncomfortable with things that were beautiful." Bochner's ideas enlivened her own, and she felt more encouraged than ever to explore the way things worked, rather than how they looked. "I was trying to find a way to tell *everything* about an object. What it was, what it might be. I wanted to make it more than an object—as if it could acquire a soul.

"That's when I started losing faith that things could be finished," she adds. "Or at least losing my interest in things that could be finished. I started making paintings that were somewhat like Abstract Expressionism, trying to put all my influences together. I had six stretchers that were five by six feet. I'd make paintings on them and show them to my graduate committee, then I'd paint them out and show the committee the next set of works. By the end of the semester they thought I had all these paintings. I *did*—I didn't mean to mislead them—but most of my stuff was covered up."

The confines of an MFA program were too small for her restless imagination. As with many young artists (and writers, in similar degree programs), school was both the best and the worst place for her to be.

Her tendency to leave things open-ended has grown even more pronounced over the years. "A couple I knew owned a painting of mine . . . every time I saw it in their living room it bothered me. Finally, I asked my friends if I could carry the piece back to my studio and tinker with it. Well, I ended up blotting it out, resurfacing it completely, and returning a painting to them that was altered beyond recognition. They complained that they had loved it the way it was. I'll never get that painting out of their house again."

The frequent pauses in Harris's speech give a listener time to study her face. It's a serious face, acutely sensitive to sights and sounds. She seems to hide behind her long, dark hair, happier observing than being observed. "Right after I got out of school, what little color I'd used just went," she says. "I was making paintings with drawing materials, mostly graphite. I stopped using canvas because I was drawing into the layers with sharp instruments and I would end up with a perforated canvas, which I thought was interesting . . . maybe I'll do that again sometime, the light coming through it was nice . . . but also I'd sand and scrape the canvas and I'd end up with rags. So I started building panels using hollow-core doors. That was really satisfying. I had all these new construction skills."

She says she'd always been impressed by the brilliant surfaces of Jasper Johns's flag paintings, and she wanted to achieve similar textures in her work. She'd heard of the encaustic process he'd used—mixing pigment with hot wax—but didn't know how to do it herself. "I tried to figure out how this was done and I learned, quickly, different ways to make really dangerous fumes," she says. "I almost blew myself up a couple of times. It's not a good idea to heat turpentine on a hot plate."

Eventually, she discovered her own cold emulsion process. "I'm surprised I haven't seen anyone else using it," she says. "It's so simple. You can buy products like it but they're incredibly expensive."

Before starting a painting she removes the stuffing of acidic paper inside the hollow core doors she buys. She covers the doors with many, many layers of gesso. This she follows with a "combination of beeswax and pigment, oil usually," she says, "sometimes mixtures I make myself with iron oxide and varnish, other materials." She has even used rust scraped from an old furnace. "I mix up several formulas and vary them and I usually don't label them so I don't know exactly what I have. It's just a game I play while I'm working." She is like a poet finding opportunities in the restrictive forms of a sonnet or a villanelle: "I establish minor obstacles for myself for the surprise. I'm always finding new things in the material. The wax makes the oil paint less predictable. I like the clumsiness of it . . . it adds to the uncertainty. Also, if I painted over something with just turpentine, it would dissolve it. But if I put on a layer of wax and then paint over it, it can be gone for much of the painting, but later, if I scrape back through it, it's still there.

"The crayon I use is a variation of a commercially available one, but chisels and whatever's lying around the studio are potential drawing instruments." She has used oil stick and pencil, engraving needles, sandpaper.

Soon after she earned her MFA, she went to work for an outreach program at the Dallas Museum of Art. Shortly thereafter, her paintings began to appear in the DW Gallery in Dallas and at the Graham and McMurtrey galleries in Houston, where reviewers noted their moodiness and luminescence. Viewers who didn't know who she was often assumed the work was done by a man. "Probably because of my name, they couldn't tell if I was a man or a woman," she says. "I was doing very large-scale things. They were big and heavy and difficult to move around and maybe some people were not used to seeing such diagrammatic drawing by a woman. But I wasn't working that way to prove a point. It was just my visual vocabulary."

She adds, "I've never tried to make conscious political or feminist statements. The idea of conventional beauty is very limiting, and that's why I've tried to eliminate it from my work, but it's a problem that transcends gender and culture."

In 1992 Harris married Dan Flavin, an artist, like Mel Bochner, slapped with the minimalist label in the 1960s (Flavin rejected the tag). Famous for his fluorescent tube sculptures, he installed a four-ton piece called *Untitled (To Tracy, to Celebrate the Love of a Lifetime)* in the Guggenheim Museum, where the wedding took place. A series of pink lights, stacked in an airy totem, stretched from the museum's ground level to the top of its rotunda. Yellow and pink tubes, alternating, shone into the museum's many alcoves. Blues, greens, and reds bathed the building's other spaces. The *New Art Examiner* called the wedding "the seminal New York event . . . [w]ith the bride in an Isaac Mizrahi dress and a bevy of art-world personalities in attendance."

The site was certainly appropriate: the swimming, circular form of the Guggenheim resembles an object in one of Harris's paintings.

Until Flavin's death in 1996, she lived with him in Wainscott, New York. Her reputation as an insightful young painter continued to grow. Lorraine Adams, a writer for the *Washington Post*, described one of her exhibitions at the Benton Gallery in Southampton as a "deeply moving history of trying to bring to light what is lost." She concluded, "[Harris] is signaling in this work that, if she can just enlarge enough, like a scientist peering through a magnificently powerful microscope, she may peer right into the mystery of death, and instead of seeing [a] muck of black . . . find an orderly, immediately understood cylinder of golden light."

In the early afternoon, Harris takes me to the Arlington Museum of Art, a former department store building between Dallas and Fort Worth now converted into a cultural Mecca. The transformation isn't quite complete; the vast, bright space is uncongenial to meditation and the contemplation of art. The curators do the best they can, though: they're convivial and ambitious. Currently, they're storing a number of Harris's paintings from a recent exhibition, and she has generously offered to unpack them and show them to me. The new paintings are light; she has learned to refine the panels so they're no longer bulky. She's a tall woman, and many of the paintings match her height. Though there are smaller pieces, she seems to work best in a large format—trying to say *everything* about an object requires a lot of space. Some of the paintings are on single panels. Others stretch across two or three sections of wood. In these, the visible seams add an extra dash of uncertainty to the objects Harris examines, undermining their stability, opening fault lines and gaps. She invites me to feel the pieces. Their surfaces, even the most harshly worked, are as soft as skin, wounded and gouged. These are sculptures as well as paintings and drawings. For all of their diagrammatic qualities, they're strangely touching. In part, their purposeful lack of finish accounts for this, emphasizing doubt, curiosity, obsession, even love. The works are also poignant because of Harris's use of color. She has limited her palette in favor of draftsmanship, but her velvet azures, candlelight ambers, wreaths of copper and watery greens are often somber, sometimes buoyant. These are the remnants of colors that might lie behind a Matisse or Bonnard interior, if the rooms were stripped to their raw nerves.

Harris admits that sometimes her own nerves nearly fray as she works. "It's a very emotional experience," she tells me. "All the things we've been talking about—philosophy, science—they're not disconnected from emotion.

"We change every day," she goes on, trying to tease out the feelings behind her work. "We resolve very few of our personal dilemmas." Sometimes the whirlpools in her pieces suggest "mental collapse, confusion."

Permutations again.

"Often when I'm working I feel horrible conflict, angst, anger, joy . . . just what it feels like to be alive."

Up close, it's easy to see how the translucent oil-and-wax mixture captures her gestures, but the paintings aren't violent like the "action" paintings of Pollock or de Kooning. Her gestures are softened, traced in the wax as lightly as memory.

"I'm interested in how time and memory affect the perception of an object," she says. Clearly, she's also fascinated by chance and its relation to vision: "When a coin falls it turns and you see one side and then the other. When a coin spins it turns into a sphere . . . all the possibilities."

This manner of seeing recalls analytical Cubism, which fragmented the world in order to view it from several angles at once, but Harris builds rather than destroys, and—unlike her minimalist mentors— adds rather than subtracts. The objects suggested in her paintings— cups, vessels, vortices; bodies, towers, screws; hurricanes, hieroglyphs, prisons—are alive: mechanical and organic, abstract and specific, blossoming and buried.

Wittgenstein once extolled the virtues of "touch[ing] everything a dozen times," a practice he followed when he worked briefly as an architect, designing his sister's house in Vienna. For hours each day, while the house was under construction, Wittgenstein's sister opened and closed doors and windows while Wittgenstein watched, tinkered, and made adjustments. He built the house as "one constructs a watch," his sister later remembered.

Similarly, Harris (an old hand at un-fixing watches) tinkers, touches, and retouches her worlds-in-progress, as her titles reveal: *Kepler's Knots, Patterns for a Measure of Language, Chronology for the Thaumatrope, Map for the Fall of a Coin, Speaking Cage, The Distance between Skin and Scar, Hydra of Expectation, The Mechanics of Vacillation, Disregarded*

*Omen, Ghost.* These sound like entries in a brilliant, slightly fevered encyclopedia lost in the labyrinths of Borges's Library of Babel.

An astronomer, madly dreaming; a spirit becoming flesh; a lover's body breaking into bloom.

Harris pauses. Then she says, "I think of the things I paint as structures and I can see them when I'm working on them. I can walk all the way around them in my mind. So what I'm doing is making an examination of a structure that doesn't really exist." Or that once existed, if only as a possibility, and continues to haunt the world. "If I wanted to make these things real, I'd work three-dimensionally. I have done drawings of things as if they were studies for something that was going to be built. Some are gravitationally possible, some aren't. It would be interesting to see if I could make one of those things. . . . It would be like building a tree from the inside out."

In the meantime, she continues to be inspired by the objects she collects—rope baskets, urns, architectural pediments, carved horns, African snuff holders, pipe fittings, a shuttle for a loom—and the objects she imagines, panicking when her dreams become too discernible. She only likes her work when she's hated it. "Things are more complete when they're incomplete," she insists, repeating that when something is too finished "it's only what it is, not what it could have been."

# The Dying Animal

I want to think about the body and the spirit, about literature's approach to spiritual experience. *Art, texts, self-reflection*, or, conversely, a passionate attachment to the *real world*—the terms of the old, hackneyed debate about the value of postmodernism's meta-language provide a good starting point for a discussion of spiritual writing.

We sometimes speak of the "body of a text" and of the "corpus of literature." Is it a stretch, then, to see arguments for or against narrative opacity as, in some sense, replicating the old Puritan uneasiness with the body, the brute carcass? In America's predominant Judeo-Christian strains, throughout the nation's history, denial of the body has been strongly encouraged. Humility and shame. Exposing one's limbs is a sin. A writer writing about writing is exposing the body of the text, flaunting its functions (nasty word!). Who wants to *watch* the linguistic intercourse necessary to make life on the page?

I'm joking and I'm not.

Texts and textual interpretation are vital to all religious traditions (think of illuminated manuscripts, whose physical page-space declared the delights and the punishments of God as powerfully as any of the *ideas* inscribed on vellum or papyrus). Debates about the substance and uses of words are as essential as fights about the duality of human nature. Body and spirit, text and content.

Thank God for the real world.

Or: In the beginning was the Word, and the Word was with God, and *was* God.

I wish to suggest that a self-reflexive narrative is essentially spiritual in nature. In purely American terms, it is rife with the paradox at the heart of Judeo-Christian attitudes toward the body.

Consider Ron Hansen's novel, *Mariette in Ecstasy* (1991). At its center is a conflict between silence and noise. Silence can only be achieved through the body's mortification. Noise is the animal's cry of glory.

A young girl, Mariette, enters a cloister, the Sisters of the Crucifixion. Early in the story, she walks to church surrounded by the clamor of her village—horses, children, friends. Though she tries to honor the Rules of Silence, acknowledging people only by "smiling or touching their wrists or fleetingly laying her hand on a baby's head," noise crowds her.

By contrast, her fellow penitents "observe a Great Silence from Compline at night until just after Mixt" each day. Prior to Mariette's arrival in the cloister, the sisters exist in a rather dull peace, their enforced humility broken now and then only when the necessities of daily life—cleaning, eating, repairing parts of the buildings—become, for one reason or another, overwhelming, provoking an outburst. For the most part, the sisters communicate using hand signs, keeping the body quiet and as still as possible. When they talk to God, they do so mentally, as though no lips graced the world, no teeth, no tongues.

Hansen's spare prose—several paragraphs consist of short, single sentences—enacts this theme of denial. Fragments and gaps trim his page-space.

Try to ignore the body.

You can't, no matter what you think.

Inevitably, belly-rumbles will break the quiet like a skit in one of Charlie Chaplin's jerky old slapstick reels. The throbbing of a stubbed toe will send tremors through the earth. Similarly, stripped-down prose. Less is more? Absolutely. No one screams louder than a minimalist.

Does this paradox explain why, in many traditions of worship, when God chooses to communicate, He does so by extremely physical means? Seizures. Stigmata. To please God, we try to refine ourselves into pure spirit. God responds with a laugh and a slap in the face, as if to remind us, Hey, don't forget you *have* a face.

It appears that Christ has embraced Mariette. She responds by slipping into trances and bleeding from her palms. She retreats into the silence of ecstasy. Still, noise envelops her: the whispering, the gos- siping of the sisters. Mother Saint-Raphael shouts irritably. Her silent authority has been rankled by the violent eruptions on the limbs of this pious young girl. Or is she faking her symptoms?

Better to veil the body? Even if God has imprinted it with His text?

By raising but refusing to answer these questions, Hansen's unset- tling novel forces us to confront *interpretation* in the fullness of its ambiguities. Heeding silence and noise, reading the texts, is always open to error. We are not saved from mistakes but at least stand vigilant if we remain acutely self-conscious and read the ways we read.

Philip Roth, that most self-conscious of writers, once entitled a book *Reading Myself and Others*. The title foregrounds the narrative energy driving most of his novels, energy pulsing from highly educated, ex- tremely self-aware narrators busily interpreting themselves and the world they inhabit, but whose minds cannot save them from the tor- ments of their bodies. If Ron Hansen sees human affairs primarily through a spiritual lens in *Mariette in Ecstasy*, Philip Roth has consis- tently insisted on the body's authority.

"No matter how much you know, no matter how much you think . . . you're not superior to sex," says David Kepesh, the narrator of Roth's *The Dying Animal* (2001). Kepesh is given to reading, to the pleasures of the mind, the richness of art, but prides himself on his pragmatism and bluntness. (He is not devoutly Jewish, but he embraces in his bones the Talmudic tradition of argument and tireless analysis.) He knows, or thinks he knows, that the body will undermine the spirit every time. Spiritual pursuits—here he would include creating and cherishing art—are elaborate games to him. They are designed to make socially palatable our ungovernable lust for one another. Kepesh lures young women to his apartment to show them the rare manuscripts he owns or to share with them reproductions of famous paintings, in preparation for springing his seductions.

*The Dying Animal* flirts with the reader, admiring its own build, as if in a mirror, flaunting its elegant form. "I'll never forget . . . I was sit- ting where you are, at the corner of the sofa," Kepesh says. Is the man addressing *me*? the reader thinks. No. It turns out, Kepesh's story is

aimed at a specific listener, someone who stays in the shadows, bodi-
less. But the confusion remains. The reader is never allowed to move
beyond the artifice of the tale. Constantly, we are reminded we are
engaging a work of art. For Kepesh (for Roth?), art is sexual dalliance.

Roth takes his title from Yeats's "Sailing to Byzantium":

> Consume my heart away; sick with desire
> And fastened to a dying animal
> It knows not what it is.

Yeats's speaker, his spirit ill with mortal hungers, imagines fashioning a different "bodily form," not "from any natural thing" but from
"armored gold and gold enameling." He imagines becoming a work of
art, a mechanical bird, "set upon a golden bough to sing . . . / Of what is
past, or passing, or to come."

Denial of the body, repugnance at time's depredations, yearning to
be immortal: Yeats posits art, not religion, as the eternal realm, the
repository of our best thoughts, made to resist the forces of aging. But
of what does art "sing"? "Of what is past, or passing, or to come." It
does not escape time. Time remains its central concern, time and all it
brings: hungers, sickness, dying.

Kepesh knows this. "No matter how much you think . . . you're not
superior to sex." Art and its airy aspirations—fine. Well and good. But
he won't try to flee the sickness of desire. Instead, he'll indulge it, with
art as the bait.

He stalks young lovers whose bodies are new to them, still being
tested, titillated. Consuela, a student of his who particularly ignites
him, is "so newly hatched as a woman that to find fragments of broken
shell adhering to that ovoid forehead wouldn't have been a surprise," he
says. "I saw right away that she was going to be my girl." She loves "all
of art," and he plays upon her aesthetic "earnestness," inviting her to his
apartment to see his large library, his piano, his art books, his "devotion
to what I do." "It is a trick," he admits.

"You could pass for a duchess," he tells her. "There must be a duchess
looking like you on the walls of the Prado. Do you know the famous
painting of Velázquez, *The Maids of Honor*?"

Down a spiral steel staircase, among his stacks of books, he locates a reproduction of the painting and teaches her aspects of its features of composition. "These are the veils of the dance," he tells his unnamed listener. He is also talking to the reader. What "you're disguising [by showing this young girl art] is the thing that got you here, the pure lust. . . . You know you want it and you know you're going to do it and nothing is going to stop you." No matter what you think.

Velázquez's *The Maids of Honor* (*Las Meninas*), painted in 1656, is notoriously self-reflexive. At its center stands the five-year-old royal princess, Infanta Margarita Teresa of Austria, child of Spain's King Philip IV. Attending her are maids of honor forming a protective retinue. This arrangement suggests that one of the painting's subjects is the sanctity and safety of childhood. Her body is still new to the princess, untouched by the world, not yet sickened with desire.

However, the painting's real interest lies elsewhere. This portrait turns the conventions of painting, as Velázquez had learned them, upside down. Traditionally, the subject of a royally commissioned portrait would be the king and/or queen. Here, Philip and his lady appear only as hazy reflections in a mirror attached to a wall behind the figure of the painter, addressing his canvas (its back to us, on its easel) next to the princess. The mirrored reflection seems to place the king and queen outside the frame, standing where *we* do as we view the painting. The painter and the princess stare at them. At us. Thus, perspective and the act of viewing become the subjects of *Las Meninas*. It is a work of art about a work of art.

So is *The Dying Animal* (Roth is this novel's King Philip). Kepesh's story, addressed to an ambiguous "you," places the reader in the body-space of a ghostly other presence, the way *Las Meninas* switches out the viewer and the monarch.

Like the figure of the painter affixed to his canvas, shaped by the strokes of his brush, Kepesh's form on the page resides in the words he speaks—of this we are repeatedly reminded. "I have to go . . . I'm going," he says on the book's final page. His listener gets the last word. "Don't," he says. "If you go, you're finished." And he is. The book ends.

This is the kind of trickery that enraged postmodernism's critics. But Roth has taken great pains to link his narrative to a broader history of art, to Velázquez and Yeats. To what purpose? These were artists rigorously contemplating the nature of the art they made in order to better understand *of what art sings*. Like Yeats, opposing immortal beauty to the "sickness of desire," and Velázquez, placing youthful innocence at the center of a meditation on power and the self, Roth pits art against sex, the body against the spirit, testing their interplay.

Kepesh calls himself a product of the sixties "revolution" in America. For him, this was a rebellion against "unquestioned superiors" whose language, he says, "could have come from St. Augustine." He shares Nathaniel Hawthorne's view of the American soul. In America, "jollity and gloom" contend "for an empire."

Politics was not the point of the sixties, pleasure was: resisting the Puritan mindset, the coming of a "sexual age when the music was changing." For *music* read *language*, the *nature of narrative*, questioning, at last, the superiors' tongues.

Ultimately, given Kepesh's nature, the subject of *The Dying Animal* is the "flesh that is born and the flesh that dies," sex as "corruption" and sex as "revenge against death." And why is a self-reflexive narrative (the "new music") appropriate for such a discussion? Conceptually, as we have seen, it privileges the body—that of the text. We are confronted with marks on a page every bit as strange and stark as wounds on the ecstatic's palms. Such marks challenge traditional authorities (hence, Mother Saint-Raphael's irritable shout when Mariette's spiritual swooning upstages her). God's favored mode of communication appears to emphasize the manner not the message. Why? No one screams louder than a minimalist.

But more to the point: inevitably, a self-examining narrative will expose its weaknesses, its inconsistencies, its frailty as a form. The limits of *how* and *how much we think* are revealed by how and how much we think.

Think about *Las Meninas.* As we view the painting, our bodies fill the king's void. Physical matter occupies the faintest trace of a spirit. In essence, a transubstantiation.

Precisely what *all* art seeks to achieve.


Near the end of *The Dying Animal,* Consuela reveals that her "gorgeous breasts," so captivating to Kepesh, are riddled with cancer. Like a camera obscura, a primitive scope channeling light and flipping an image upside down, the novel reverses our expectations. Kepesh, rapidly aging, remains healthy and strong. It is the newly hatched young lady who is dying. *Hers* is the flesh betrayed. Doctors order her to have a mastectomy. Like Mariette, she will become a text of wounds, the tragic nature of which is difficult to grasp.

On the eve of her surgery, she asks Kepesh to photograph her breasts. She would like a record of her body as Kepesh knew and worshiped it. Kepesh worries that a peeping tom (someone akin to the reader), would interpret his motives as pornographic. He approaches the scene as if through a mirrored lens: pornography becomes its opposite. The moment swells with tender affection.

Kepesh does not develop the photographs. He fears the prurience of professional developers, and he possesses no dark room skills. Materially, Consuela's vibrant body disappears. In Kepesh's mind it remains fixed for a time like Velázquez's beautiful princess, the sanctity of her youth preserved (or lost?) amid nagging questions of perspective.


"Of what is past, or passing, or to come": narratives are time-bound, trapped in duration, linked to movement. Left to right, right to left (as in reading the Talmud), horizontal and vertical. *The body of the text* is not a metaphor. Texts have the *properties* of bodies.

Like bodies, texts shelter the spirit, just as the brains in our skulls box up memories, voices, images witnessed and imagined.

In certain religions, the spirit is tainted by contact with the flesh that dies; thus, hatred of the body. And yet isn't flesh ennobled by contact with the spirit?

Which image is right? How will we know unless we peer through the scope and examine the very nature of image making?

Is the world "real"? Or is the world, rather, *fashioned* by the Word?

Either way, it is passing, dying animal. No matter what you think.

# PART TWO

# Imagination's Relationship to the World

# Dante's Astronomer

In 1920 T. S. Eliot complained that the astronomical "scaffold" in Dante's *Divine Comedy* was "almost unintelligible." Eliot saw Dante's stars as part of an allegorical "presence" in the writing that guided readers to the *Comedy*'s emotional core—an absorption "into the divine," he said, based on the study of spiritual laws. To appreciate the poem, it was not necessary to measure Dante's universe, Eliot wrote; one need only glimpse it, the way one catches faint starlight by glancing away from the source.

Ten years before Eliot aired his complaint a self-educated amateur astronomer named Mary Ackworth Evershed sat on a hill in southern India, seven thousand feet above sea level, staring at the daylight moon as she grappled with apparent mistakes in Dante's cosmos. The Aristotelian-Ptolemaic structure on which Dante based his universe had long been discredited, but that wasn't the sort of error absorbing her. Precision was her concern. Further, she wanted to enter Dante's literary imagination, to determine if he was accurate *within* his conception. Was he, as Eliot would claim, "unintelligible" on the subject of astronomy? Or was he, for a man of his time and place, as insightful as one could be about the sky?

The moon tugged at Mary Evershed and stirred the twin tides of her passions: poetry and science. Dante was the poet who most thrilled her; as a long-time stargazer, and the wife of an observatory official, she couldn't just skim Dante's cosmography. The *Comedy* mentions stars fifty-five times, with numerous other references to the moon and planets, to the constellations, and to seasonal measurements. As she watched the day-moon set, she recalled Dante's little-known Latin treatise the "Questo de Aqua et Terra," in which he appeared to make a troubling lunar blunder.

In the "Questo," Dante argues that the moon is always in perigee (that is, at its closest approach to earth) near the earth's southern hemisphere. In fact, medieval scientists knew the moon's perigee shifted along the zodiac, north *and* south of the equator. Dante's assertion seemed sloppy—in which case the *Comedy's* scaffolding might very well contain loose steps.

(His slip appears in a larger treatise *we* know to be scientifically unfounded, but that was beside the point—*fantastical precision* was part of Dante's charm.)

The "Questo" insists that land exists only in the earth's northern hemisphere, with the exception of the island-mountain Purgatory. Dante wonders how this could occur, geologically. Did the moon's "elevational influence" wrench mountains out of the ocean? Certainly not, Dante writes. Everyone knows the moon's "influence" is stronger in the south, and yet it produced little territory there. Some other force must have accounted for Purgatory. (The assertion that land exists only in the northern hemisphere is not Dante's private misconception: it was the accepted Aristotelian view of his day.)

Pondering all this, Mary closed her notebook, which she'd filled with sketches of the moon and observations about the nature and color of the evening sky. The moon vanished beneath the Palani Hills. Mary stood and brushed grass from her ankle-length skirt. As she would later write of this day, Dante's error disconcerted her. Still, the joy she felt at living on a mountaintop near a state-of-the-art observatory, with time at the end of each evening to read and think about poetry, overwhelmed her. Her only irritation was the lack of books out here— studies of medieval history that might help her determine how much of existence Dante got right. Within a few months, she would begin to compose the finest book ever written on Dante's science, and a most unusual examination of poetic imagination.

The Palani Hills rise above waterfall-filled forests and lakes in southern India where plums and plantains grow alongside rare kurinji flowers that bloom once every twelve years. Kodaikanal, the name of the region, is Tamil for "Gift of the Forest." For Mary Evershed, the landscape's mirroring of Dante's geography, which helped her visualize the Pilgrim's trek as she reread the *Comedy*, was indeed a gift. The Kukkal Cave mouths, rough, overhanging outcrops in a pine and wattle forest flush with geraniums, wild orchids, and leeches the size of a man's back, formed the Inferno's maw. Gentle, glittering ponds on evergreen slopes recalled *Purgatorio*'s opening lines, in which the poet sails the "small bark" of his wit on smooth waters beneath a sapphire-colored sky. And when Mary hiked past temples humming with prayerful chants, reached the top of the hills' highest peak, jutting through rain-fed streams, and came to the Kodaikanal solar research center, she felt she had glimpsed the Empyrean.

Her unlikely presence in this spot was the result of a pilgrimage that—while strictly earthbound—was almost as miraculous as Dante's in his poem. Born on the first day of the year in 1867, in Plymouth Hoe, England, she was educated entirely at home. Her father, Andrew Orr, an artillery officer, didn't value formal schooling; on the other hand, he also didn't think girls should be treated any differently than boys. Mary and her little sister, Lucy, were given as much access as their brothers to the harsh governesses that dispensed the family lessons (there were seven children in all, including two older sisters). Mary's father died when she was three; soon afterward, Mary's mother, Lucy, took her sons and daughters to live with Lucy's father, a clergyman in a country vicarage near Bath. A young governess, a Miss Hawar, assumed responsibility for the children's mental development. Mary, whom the family called Mindie, loved Miss Hawar. For the next nine years, she lapped up whatever the young woman said. This was the full extent of Mary's schooling. After that, she was on her own.

Victorian academics had long extolled the virtues of Italian literature. Dante was well known to British school children. When Mary was twenty, she and her sister Lucy traveled to Florence to extend their educations. They visited the Baptistry, where Dante had rested his head against the wall (Mary confessed to her sister how terribly moved she was that Dante, in exile, longed to see his beloved Baptistry just once more, a wish he was never granted). In the Bargello she stared at the intelligent young face, modeled on Dante's, in Giotto's portrait of souls in Paradise. Mary stood as if waiting for Dante to speak to her. John Ruskin had written that, of all poets, Dante was the most sensitive to light's effects on the eye. If Dante could say anything at all to Mary, she wished it could be an explanation of the light, so much more intense in Italy than it was back home. She was as struck by Florence's sky as she was by its buildings, streets, and bridges.

Three years later, the sky impressed her again when she, young Lucy, and their mother joined an older sister in Australia, where the sister had settled in marriage. Australia's best-known astronomer, John Tebbut, ran a private observatory in Windsor, New South Wales, near the Orrs' house. Tebbut had discovered the Great Comets of 1861 and 1881. Mary made regular visits to his observatory. Impressed by her insightful questions, he encouraged her in her studies of the stars.

In 1866 the British science publisher James Gall had printed a pocket-sized book with simple maps of northern constellations. Mary had used Gall's book to learn her way around the northern sky. No similar volume existed for the southern hemisphere. Mary began to document her observations and to plan charts of Australia's stars, modeled on Gall's maps. Her purpose, she told Tebbut, was to get "people (children and adults) on the track of observing for themselves the movements of the heavenly bodies." In 1895 Gall & Inglis, by now a well-known, if specialized, publishing firm, agreed to print Mary's work and produced gorgeous, deep-blue maps of the stars, all in a circular shape as if seen through a telescope. Mary called the book *An Easy Guide to Southern Stars* and published it under the gender-neutral name of M. A. Orr. She convinced Tebbut to provide a preface, hoping his blessing would get the book noticed. Though he states his "pleasure in commending this little work," his condescension toward Mary as an amateur and a woman is apparent in the preface's brevity and thrust. "The whole of my spare time being absorbed in astronomical work of a technical character," Tebbut writes, "I have not had the opportunity for going into a detailed examination of the contents, but I believe we may safely trust the accuracy of the enterprising authoress. The work is pleasantly written."

In any event, the book sold moderately well. Mary's enthusiasm for the history of astronomy, the lore of star names, and the joy of observing the constellations' "most graceful shapes" proved irresistible to those who came across the volume.

By now, Mary was reading Dante in Italian. She carried the *Comedy* with her wherever she went. She told her sisters that in the vast dust-plains of the Australian Outback she got a sense of Dante's exile, the arduousness of wandering from city to city. Her initial unfamiliarity with the southern sky helped her see the sky anew, as though she were witnessing stars for the very first time. These were the constellations Dante the Pilgrim saw, emerging from Purgatory "pure" and "remade" and "prepared to rise up to the stars."

As early as 1896, Mary started wrestling with astral problems in Dante. In a tiny notebook she sketched the positions of the sun, moon, and stars as Dante described them. Of line 64 in the fourth canto of *Purgatorio*, "il Zodiaco rubecchio," she wonders if Dante means "the zodiac" has been "reddened by the sun" or if he is pointing out a red-hued patch of the "zodiacal cogwheel." Elsewhere, she worries that, while mapping Paradise, Dante has forgotten the equinox. In *Paradiso's* third canto, Dante calls the sphere of the moon the "slowest" in the heavens. Mary can't determine if this is a reference to the moon's size or diurnal motion. In an agitated hand, she returns to *Purgatorio*, where Dante suggests that, from a particular position in the sky, the sun "lights alternatively each hemisphere." It would be more accurate, Mary writes, to say that it "lights the starry heavens above and earth and three planets below." Dante had found his astronomer.

In Mary Evershed's lifetime, British women who wished to become professional astronomers encountered numerous barriers. To begin with, astronomy was not taught as a stand-alone discipline in British universities. It was a branch of mathematics and physics. At Cambridge, women were allowed to take examinations but could not earn degrees until 1923, and they could not become full members of the university until 1948. A woman with her head in the stars could only hope for a menial position as a "computer" in an observatory—often some wretched colonial outpost in the middle of nowhere—compiling tedious numbers as parts of research projects for which she would never be credited.

Women fared no better in elite U.S. universities. Typical of this period was Harvard College Observatory's policy of paying its "computers" twenty-five cents an hour. On more than one occasion, Harvard hired partially deaf women, perhaps believing they were free of distractions from their tasks. Regularly, the university received shipments of heavy photographic plates taken in the Peruvian Andes, hauled by mules across rickety suspension bridges, and transported by boat and train. In Harvard Square the glass plates were mounted on wooden viewing frames and, later, turned over to the computers to calculate the relative brightness of the tiny star images.

Internationally, women had no choice but to be amateurs, in the tradition of Caroline Herschel, sister of William, who discovered the planet Uranus. In the 1780s, when William sacrificed a music career to manufacture telescopes, Caroline became his assistant, polishing lenses and jotting down night-sky observations. On her own, she discovered eight comets. After William's death in 1822, she compiled a catalog of nebulae that William's son John used to advance his career as a scientist, though he never gave Caroline credit.

In the early nineteenth century, children—and especially girls—became enamored of a series of constellation cards peddled under the name Urania's Mirror in England. The cards showed the major constellations with punched-out holes in place of the stars. When held against a light, the holes (of various sizes, to indicate stellar magnitudes) could dazzle a child's eyes. Urania's Mirror had been devised by an unidentified "lady"—she is referenced in a popular book of the day, Jehosaphat Aspin's *A Familiar Treatise on Astronomy* (1825)—a savvy amateur whose name may never be known to us.

Among women in pursuit of the sky, sunspots and solar flares were favorite objects of study. Elizabeth Brown, a tireless amateur, suggested that sunspot drawing was a perfect activity for "ladies" because they had plenty of time to devote to it and needed only a dark glass, a pencil, and paper to do the work. Perhaps most importantly, their delicate constitutions could avoid exposure to the chilling night air.

(Brown had literary ambitions, publishing books about the sun—anonymously, so they'd be taken seriously—under the slightly lurid titles *In Pursuit of a Shadow* and *Caught in the Tropics*. Generally, science books written by or addressed to women were dismissed by professionals as "popular" and therefore unworthy. One of the best known of these books was J. P. Nichol's *View of the Architecture of the Heavens* [1839], subtitled, "A Series of Letters to a Lady." Among others, George Eliot was smitten by Nichol's work; she said it freed her imagination to "behold . . . floating worlds.")

Another reason for the sun's popularity among amateurs was the social opportunities provided by eclipse expeditions. Various clubs for amateur sky gazers, from the Liverpool Astronomical Society to the British Astronomical Association, sponsored journeys to various hilltops to observe and record solar eclipses. Walter Maunder, a Fellow of the Royal Astronomical Society, was instrumental in starting the BAA in 1890, in part because the RAS's exclusion of women so offended him.

Physical astronomy was a field in which amateurs and professionals could happily meet. Professionals had access to sophisticated equipment, while the amateurs had a large rank and file and an eagerness to watch the sky for hours on end. At meetings of the BAA, the eager amateur Mary Ackworth Orr met the budding young professional John Evershed. The sun—a dollop of Dante's Divine Light—sparked their courtship, as they traveled together to Norway, India, and Algiers, chasing eclipses.

In August 1896 John and Mary joined fifty-eight others, all of whom paid their own way, on an expedition sponsored by the British Astronomical Association to Vadsø Island, Norway, to see the total eclipse. Annie Maunder, Walter's wife, a dedicated amateur who would become one of Mary's best friends, later reported that "unfortunate" weather on August 9, the day of the eclipse, scuttled "those scientific fruits which had been hoped for" from the day. However, the trip was "most successful" at cementing bonds among the observers. We may imagine that among the things John observed was Mary's demure smile, and her dark eyebrows, often quizzically raised, which gave her a delighted but slightly melancholy look under straight brown hair. A keen observer, Mary must have noted John's square jaw, high forehead, and gentle mouth, held tight. He had an astonishing stamina for craning his head to the sky.

On May 28, 1900, the BAA's plans to send a large party to Algiers, where the eclipse would be total, fell through when the ship the group had chartered from the Royal Mail Stream Packet Company was requisitioned by the British government. The government needed a vessel to run unspecified cargo to and from South Africa.

We know from a rather dry paper John delivered to the Royal Astronomical Society on July 16 that he and his brother Harry made it to Algiers, and to the nearby countryside, to photograph the sun's flash spectrum. Barbara Reynolds, a noted Dante scholar who came into possession of Mary's papers after her death in 1949, writes that somehow Mary also reached Algiers. The papers suggest she traveled with four other women from the BAA, lugging with her a three-inch refracting telescope, and that the women commandeered the rooftop of the British Consul's villa as an observation post.

It's likely that John spent time with Mary in Algiers before setting off into the country, and that he rejoined Mary's group once the eclipse was over. John's mission had been funded by a government body whose title might, in an ideal world, describe *all* bureaucratic entities—The Permanent Eclipse Committee. Even though John and Mary were miles apart at the precise moment the moon approached the sun, they had journeyed far together with a common purpose. The shared adventure was heady, perhaps even transcendent, as the name of John's endeavor suggested: The Expedition to the South Limit of Totality.

How does one ever return from that? A lifetime romance had begun.

John Evershed was born at Gomshall in Surrey in 1864. He came from a long line of farmers who trusted the stars' seasonal signs for planting and harvesting; his maternal great-grandfather ran a shop in Portsmouth for selling nautical charts and almanacs. Initially educated by private tutors and teachers at a Unitarian preparatory school, John eventually attended classes at Croydon, where, he said, "by a lucky accident I passed the only examination I have ever been subjected to."

As a boy, he was enchanted by a partial eclipse of the sun, which he had seen through a local doctor's telescope. In the library, he studied eclipse records, such as the Syrian account of 1375 B.C.: "The sun was put to shame and went down in daytime." Astronomers were romantic figures for him (as Dante well understood, a strong kinship exists between scientific and literary imaginations). When John was six, he had seen pictures in an illustrated broadsheet of Paris under a barrage of German shells, and he read how the French astronomer Janssen escaped the city in a hot-air balloon to observe a total solar eclipse.

Through his eldest brother, a student at London's School of the Mines, he met Raphael Meldola, a Fellow of the Royal Society, who in turn introduced John to Charles Darwin. John's romance with science grew. By the time he was thirteen, he was making his own telescopes using discarded opera glasses and toy prisms. Through the prisms he saw the solar spectrum split into two fine lines, a glimpse into hidden worlds determining his life's path.

For a while he went to work for a chemical manufacturer, but by 1890 his interest in the sun had led him to establish his own observatory at Kenley in Surrey, where he built a spectroscope, set up an eighteen-inch reflecting telescope, and began to photograph solar activity (as a sidelight, he also took brilliant color photos of butterflies). Formally, his training in astronomy was not much more extensive than Mary's, but a man was expected to pursue a career.

John and Mary lived apart for the five years following their Algiers expedition, but they saw each other often. John returned to his observatory in Kenley. Mary spent this period in nearby Frimley, Surrey. She set up her own observatory with the refractor she had taken to Algiers and focused her attention on the moon and variable stars (stars whose light output changes because of eclipses, unusual rotation, or physical shifts such as swelling or shrinking). Mary read more about the history of astronomy. She remained active in the BAA, one of whose members, Agnes Clerke, twenty-five years Mary's senior, became a cherished friend. In addition to being a skilled astronomer, Agnes was a renowned historian and a fellow admirer of Dante (she had also, as a child, taken piano lessons in Dublin from the women on whom James Joyce based the spinster aunts in his short story "The Dead"). As a young woman, she had lived in Florence for seven years, and Mary loved to compare memories with her of Dante's youthful haunts.

In 1904 Mary published a paper, "Variable Stars of Long Period," in the *Journal of the British Astronomical Association.* Her focused work shows a desire to pursue a professional career—and perhaps indicates an assertion of independence, a friendly competition with John, who was busy on his solar studies down the road.

Edmund T. Whittaker, a mathematician at Cambridge and Secretary of the Royal Astronomical Society, had married a cousin of Mary's. Early in 1906 he was appointed Professor of Astronomy at Trinity College Dublin and Director of Dunsink Observatory. He planned an intensive study of red stars, many of which were variables, using photographs taken with a fifteen-inch reflecting telescope. Mary's knowledge of variables made her useful to him; he invited her to Ireland to live with his family in the observatory residence. Unfortunately, he told her, she would not be paid for her work. She could only come as a volunteer.

Around this time—early 1906—John received an invitation to become assistant director of the Kodaikanal Observatory in India's Dindigul District. Suddenly, John and Mary's time together, their productive rivalry, was ending. The Dunsink opportunity didn't appeal to Mary, but the move would give her access to fine equipment. Professionally, John could hardly refuse the opening he'd been offered. He seems to have been stunned by the possibility that he might lose Mary. He asked her to marry him and come with him to the Palani Hills.

She had little time to sort through her personal and professional urgings. To advance as an astronomer, she could work unpaid as her cousin-in-law's "computer," or be the trailing spouse of an observatory's assistant director. Either way, she lost her independence. On the other hand, to refuse either option might be to ignore the only paths available to her, aside from staying where she was.

The history of nineteenth-century British astronomy is replete with examples of husband and wife teams, such as Walter and Annie Maunder and William and Margaret Huggins, whose distaff side failed to earn equal credit for research and publishing, despite clear evidence of shared work.

On September 4, 1906, at St. Mary's Parish Church, Cloughton, near Scarborough in Yorkshire, Mary Orr married John Evershed. Mary was thirty-nine.

In one of the most celebrated passages in *Inferno*, in canto 5, deep in a place where no stars shine, Francesca de Rimini confesses to Dante that she and her lover, Paolo, were overcome by lust after a spell of "reading" together led their "eyes to meet." At first blush, John and Mary appear to have little in common with Paolo and Francesca, except that their love blossomed over "reading"—in their case, a common intellectual endeavor, deciphering patterns in the sky and poring over books and charts. Like Dante's pair, John and Mary managed to "move through the air," borne "forward" on powerful wills to work, and their wedding could have been blessed by Dante's words: "He / who rules the universe . . . / we . . . pray to Him to give you peace."

The Kodaikanal Observatory, only five years old in 1906, was one of a series of English outposts established in southern India so that, as official word had it, "posterity may be informed a thousand years hence of the period when mathematical sciences were first planted by British liberality in Asia." A more pragmatic reason for constructing the observatories was to monitor the weather and to study monsoon patterns, so British properties here could be better protected in the future.

Before settling at Kodaikanal, John and Mary visited several observatories in the United States and Asia, so John could get up to snuff on worldwide solar research. The couple spent a month in California, at Mount Wilson where John studied George Ellery Hale's spectroheliograph, a device for scanning the sun's image through moving slits, which isolates a portion of the spectrum and lets the observer analyze the chemical composition of the sun's gases. John made mental notes for constructing an improved version of the instrument.

Afterward, the Eversheds traveled to Japan and eventually made it to India. They moved into the small, spare residential quarters at the top of Observatory Hill, surrounded from below by temples and farms (whose patterned fields recalled, to Mary, the agricultural glories of the *Georgics*), and above by Divine Light.

John refined the installation's spectroheliograph into the finest of its kind, surpassing Hale's model at Mount Wilson. He began a program of photographing sunspots and solar prominences, an uninterrupted collection of observations that continues to this day and forms a unique record of solar activities.

At the time, sunspots confounded astronomers. Eventually, Hale would prove them to be centers of strong magnetic fields on the sun, but for now John agreed with his friends Walter and Annie Maunder that "we may never know" what sunspots are, "for their cause seems to lie deep down in the sun itself." Do sunspots, like whales in the ocean, swim just below the sun's surface, then breach the plain of fire? We can "know . . . a whale [again] if it has a harpoon driven into it," wrote the Maunders, "but how are we to know a Sunspot when it emerges again from the solar depths?"

On January 7, 1909, John noticed on a spectrograph a radial movement of matter in the penumbral region of a sunspot—a wavelength shift indicating an outflow of gas. He searched for and confirmed the existence of similar motion in other sunspots: it became known as the Evershed Effect, a still-puzzling aspect of the sun's dynamics.

At a steady rate he published papers in the same dry prose that characterized his eclipse report to the Royal Astronomical Society. But as time went on, a curious quality crept into his writing. Was it . . . poetry?

In one report, John switched suddenly from a rote discussion of "absorption hypotheses" to a meditation on sunspots' "smoke-like veils." His 1910 remarks on Halley's Comet began with equations about the comet's "relative speed of approach" to the earth, moved into praise of the tail's "magnificent spectacle," then into a description of the "square of Pegasus, which was filled" with the comet's "faint light."

A 1917 report on the "Results of Prominence Observations" includes this remarkable paragraph:

> Day after day, sitting quietly in his own observatory, the astronomer can see the wonderfully varied forms of . . . huge flames, can measure their motions, and investigate their composition. Nothing can be more entrancing than to gaze at a great cloud, glowing as if with sunset colour, and full of intricate detail, which slowly changes, and presently grows dim and fades away, or to watch a number of fine sharp rays which shoot up, curl over, and disappear, while others take their place. In photographs, the colour and brilliance is missing, but the forms lose nothing of their strangeness and beauty.

It is clear, in comparing this passage with John's earlier work, that this is not his writing. Finally, before releasing the 1917 report to the public, he gave his wife full co-authorship credit. With earlier papers, it's difficult to say how or to what degree collaboration occurred, but at the very least we see a meeting of minds, a fruitful conversation, a melding of poetry and science.

Following her article on variable stars, Mary published in the *Monthly Notices of the Royal Astronomical Society* a significant paper on solar flares—which owed much to her husband's observations with the spectroheliograph. She was trying hard to find her place as an amateur with gifts as strong as those of professionals. Her contribution to the 1917 report, combining history with detailed observations and a poetic flair, indicated a path her writing might follow. In the meantime, she indulged the other great passion of her life: reading Dante. She recalled the pleasure she had taken in preparing *An Easy Guide to Southern Stars*, returning, mentally, to the moment when the sky became fresh to her once more—an echo of *Purgatorio's* final lines, when Dante sees the stars anew just as he is poised to enter Paradise.

For readers of English, the definitive account of Dante's astronomy, until 1903, was Edward Moore's investigation of the subject in the third volume of his *Studies in Dante*. Moore acknowledges the complexities that drove T. S. Eliot batty a few years later. He says, "It is a matter of regret that even students of ability and culture often refuse so much as to attempt to understand Dante's astronomical references. They assume ... that they are not to be understood at all, or at least not without special astronomical or mathematical training."

In his illustrious career, Moore wrote studies of Aristotle's *Ethics* and *Poetics*, and he established himself as perhaps the finest nineteenth-century authority on *The Divine Comedy*, editing the comprehensive *Oxford Dante*. Mary knew his work well.

He establishes that, in reading Dante, one accepts the earth as the cosmos' center. Surrounding it are the crystalline planetary spheres, appearing to move separately from one another against the fixed stars. That Dante uses astronomy *metaphorically* and *poetically*—sometimes at the expense of observational accuracy—is undeniable. That he means to call the reader's attention to parallels between the spheres' harmonic structures and his own poetic outline is also plain.

Moore emphasizes the *Comedy*'s allegorical beginning: "Midway along the journey of our life / I woke to find myself in some dark woods." As his travels proceed, the Pilgrim emerges as more than just a faceless Everyman. He is Dante, specific to a time and place (time measured astronomically in the poem, most often). He is named directly—just once—in *Purgatorio* 30:55, when Beatrice admonishes him not to weep over Virgil's disappearance. Moore suggests—and Mary would agree—that astronomy in the *Comedy* should be read like the Pilgrim's character development: as spiritual allegory underpinned by the educational rigor specific to Dante's era.

Moore spends much of his time deciphering Dante's seasonal measurements. For example, in *Purgatorio* 32, Dante speaks of "trees on earth" when the "strong rays fall, mingled with the light / that glows behind the heaven of the fish."

Aries is the constellation glowing behind Pisces, that is, the "heaven of the fish." When the sun is in Aries, its "strong rays" falling, the trees begin to "swell."

"This amounts to saying that the buds begin to swell at the end of March, and the flowers to come out in early April," Moore explains. He concedes that Dante may be "hard," but "he is seldom, if indeed ever, 'obscure.'" No writer "ever had more entirely clear ideas on every subject on which he speaks," Moore says. "In theology, in scholastic philosophy, in metaphysical, moral, and physical science, and in classical literature, if judged by the standard even of a contemporary specialist in each, he will not be found wanting." Dante's knowledge is "extensive," "varied," and "profound."

Though Mary appreciated Moore's work on Dante, she did not slavishly accept his interpretations. She read Dante closely, in English and Italian, and drew her own conclusions. She was a fastidious recorder of celestial phenomena. More than anything else, she shared with her poet a passion for *observational* astronomy.

She knew that Dante's excessive reading had weakened his eyes. In the *Convivio*, he writes that stars looked as blurry to him as inked letters bleeding into a damp page. Still, no one studied the world around him more keenly, and if, in the "Questo," he seemed to make a "sad" mistake about the moon, it was not sloppiness on his part: it was his thorough absorption of the ninth-century Arab astronomer Alfraganus, a major source of Dante's celestial knowledge to whom the mistake could *really* be laid. It was he who said the moon's perigee was always in the south. In her notebook, Mary wrote that the lunar circles of Ptolemy, described by Alfraganus, are complicated; but this is no surprise since the moon's motion is, in fact, *very* complicated. She found it remarkable that the irregularities caused by the elliptical form of the moon's orbit had been observed, and a geometrical system invented to represent them, however mistakenly, as early as the second century A.D.

Satisfied that her poet's scientific integrity remained intact—he was only following his most reliable sources—she reviewed the other entries she had made in her notebook concerning Dante. His curiosity, his *companionship* consoled her. He had once written that he could endure exile from Florence because he was able to gaze upon the "mirror of the sun and stars and contemplate, under any sky, the sweetest truths." On her hilltop in India, far from home, from other women of her station, she could understand the exile's dilemmas and delights. She could appreciate the nomad's rage for order—the way he had constructed his poem as a Memory Palace, a Gothic cathedral: *Inferno* with its gargoyles; the pristine ornamentation of *Purgatorio*; the stained-glass dazzle of *Paradiso*, winding ever upwards. (It did not escape her that many observatories are similarly designed: the writhing cables and howling machinery on the ground floor, untouched by natural light; above this, the telescope platform, scaled to obtain better sight; and finally the great, majestic doors of the dome—when they open, the stars rush in ...)

Perhaps, Mary decided, a study of the *Comedy's* heavens, surpassing Moore's effort, would tap her astronomical knowledge in a useful way, combine it with her literary sensibility, and offer her an excuse to plunge deeper into the pleasures of reading.

One night, she shared her insights about the "Questo" with her husband. In December 1911 a small article on the "Questo" appeared in a magazine called *The Observatory*: "Dante and Medieval Astronomy." The byline read M. A. and J. Evershed.

Eventually, John conceded Dante to his wife. As he snapped pictures of solar flares, Mary settled into a routine of deciphering Dante, communing across time with him through the shared pleasure of sky gazing. His "problem[s]" were "much on [her] mind," she writes, as she helped her husband prepare photographic equipment "in beautiful early dawns."

What is it about Dante that inclines readers to take his science so seriously? Mary put her finger on his intellectual charm. Dante's description of "celestial matter," she writes, is "one of the finest instances of his faithfulness to the teachings of astronomy as he had learned it." In *Paradiso* 2, using his "poetical imagination," he examines pearl-like, "polished" ether, a substance "soft as cloud but hard as diamond," which "offers no more resistance to Dante as he enters into it than does water to a ray of light." In passages such as this, Dante uses science and "material facts (as he conceived them) to present an allegory of the deepest religious mysteries." Time and again, if Dante's "premises be granted, the conclusions are correct," Mary says. "As regards sun, moon, and planets," they are often "correct even from the point of view of modern knowledge."

Dante's rigor, and his insistence on specificity even within a dubious framework, seduces readers into casting off what they know, to think in *his* terms.

Like Mary, Dante was most intrigued by the sun—as a Florentine, he had the "true southerner's love" of light: it is the "bringer of warmth and comfort," a sign of "renewed hope and confidence," Mary wrote. Under the sun's rays, "the rose expands, the air is gladdened, mists are dispelled, snow melts, and all things are quickened into life."

Moreover, "Dante seems to have taken some trouble to find out the exact period of the sun's revolution," Mary says. "His text-book, the *Elementa* of Alfraganus, only gives it as 365 ¼ days nearly . . . but Dante wished to be more exact, and somehow contrived to obtain a value which was much nearer the modern estimate of 365 days, 5 hours, 48 minutes, 46 seconds."

Dante must never have seen a solar eclipse, for there is "no allusion [in the *Comedy*] to the features which chiefly strike modern astronomers—the pearly corona, and blood-red prominences standing out like flames round the black disc."

Mary notes approvingly that, throughout the *Comedy*, Beatrice speaks with stunning "scientific precision." Unlike most writers, who "remember imperfectly" what they see of the sky, "or draw upon their imagination without any knowledge of celestial movements," Dante takes great care to avoid incongruities. For writers, the "moon is especially a stumbling block," Mary says, "and it is quite a rare thing for a modern novelist to introduce one without making it do something impossible. A new moon will rise at midnight, or a waning moon at sunset." Dante's moon "does indeed give us a little trouble once or twice, but he never makes flagrant mistakes of this kind."

He is not a singer of lunar light. The moon "means a loss of starlight, which he dearly loved." Mary could have been speaking of herself; as she studied and wrote, her kinship with Dante grew.

She was particularly pleased with his southern skies: accurately, "he does not place any single bright star to mark the south pole," she wrote. In *Purgatorio* 24, he mentions four bright southern stars "non viste mai fuor che alla prima gente"—never seen by anyone except the first people. Scholars have long debated the identity of these stars, and many readers have concluded that Dante is fictionalizing here. Mary says, "It is a fact that there are four bright stars in the form of a cross, lying between 56 degrees and 63 degrees south"; though they "were not recognized as a separate constellation until the beginning of the sixteenth century, when Amerigo Vespucci described them in his letters," she speculates that Dante saw or heard about these stars from travelers. She provides a map "showing what stars would have been visible to Dante at the supposed latitude of Purgatory, when Pisces was on the eastern horizon, as described in *Purgatorio* 1."

From time to time, Mary's precise modern methods catch Dante in "little inaccuracies," but overall she finds him remarkable in his "consistency and truth of description."

She concludes that the astronomical alignments in the poem do not match the real look of the sky in 1300, the year of Dante the Pilgrim's journey; for example, in 1300, the moon was not full on the night between Thursday and Good Friday, as Dante implies. He is off by a whopping three days! But Mary argues that Dante is intent on showing how *all* dates, calendars, and means of marking time are highly contingent, based on our imperfect understanding of heavenly movements.

Ultimately, the "heavens are the same to our eyes as to Dante's," Mary says. Though the "ideas suggested" by celestial bodies are "widely different" to us than they were to the poet, our universe is still "vague, vast, mysterious, without known limits or centre, offering problem after problem to the thinker." Therefore, we "share the feeling of our medieval forefathers, of the ancient Greeks, of the earliest men whenever and wherever they became men. The unerring courses of the stars speak to us . . . of perfect harmony."

The sun seems to have settled down, some, while Mary wrote her book: John notes that "not a single northern spot has been seen" on the sun's surface "from January to November 1912," and solar prominences were few in 1913. If, during this period, the observatory's plates had "traced beautiful fountain jets" of fire, Mary might have had difficulty concentrating on her manuscript, but the heavens cooperated with her project.

Twice, John left her alone to set up camp in the Valley of Kashmir. He found the solar definition extremely good there, eight thousand feet above sea level, where locals cultivated rice. Mary read, wrote, drew maps based on Dante's details, and corresponded with prominent Dante scholars, including G. V. Schiaparelli, a well-known medievalist. Though astronomy was the focus of her study, her ultimate goal was to celebrate Dante's poetry. "No one will dispute a poet's right to arrange the skies as he thinks fit," she wrote. She put the observatory staff to work, checking her interpretations of the poem against the staff's readings. Her sister Lucy arrived to help with the indexing, and Mary dedicated the book to her.

Gall & Inglis published *Dante and the Early Astronomers* in 1914. As science historian Mary Bruck says, "The circumstances of its publication were . . . unfavourable: the author was back in India, cut off by the First World War." Students of literature "were not likely to come across the catalogue of a scientific publisher. It was to be over thirty years before the book came to the notice of Dante scholars." Only two reviews of the book appeared in the science press, a note in *The Observatory* calling it "charming," and a full-page consideration in *Nature*, lauding Mary's valuable contribution to historians of science.

Quietly, Mary returned to the task of helping her husband. Using his photographs, she classified solar prominences into active and eruptive types, tracked sunspot motions, and recorded more than sixty thousand prominence observations over an eleven-year sunspot cycle. Her work at Kodaikanal, says Bruck, was a "precursor" of "cine-photography with the coronograph, a technique then far in the future."

As the observatory director, John was more and more engaged in administrative jobs. The influenza outbreak of 1918 took the life of one of his best assistants, and a replacement was tough to find. In 1923, longing to resume full-time observational astronomy, he retired as the director of Kodaikanal, and he and Mary returned to England. On their final trip from the observatory to the harbor, where they'd board a ship home, a tiger bounded across a back road in front of their car: the first wild cat they had seen in sixteen years in India.

Despite her isolation in the east, Mary considered her years in the Palani Hills the happiest of her life.

In Ewhurst, Surrey, John set up a private observatory and for the next thirty years continued his observations of the sun. By now, the Royal Astronomical Society had opened its doors to women, and Mary was elected to serve on its library committee. For the British Astronomical Society, she organized a Historical Section "to study the history of astronomy and to co-operate in research, helping to bring new facts to light and unearthing facts now buried in old books and papers." At the time, academia did not recognize the history of science as a formal branch of knowledge. Mary's most ambitious project with the Historical Section was a listing of every person for whom lunar formations had been named, a directory entitled *Who's Who in the Moon.*

Before her health began to fail, she and John made trips to Australia, Greece, and remote parts of England to watch solar eclipses, reliving their first trips together; each time, the weather spoiled their views of the sun. Mary died at home in 1949 at the age of eighty-three.

John published an article, "Recollections of Seventy Years of Scientific Work," in a magazine called *Vistas in Astronomy* in 1955, the year before he died. Without Mary's suggestions, her poetic eye and corrections of his prose, his sentences lie flat on the page, as they did in his earliest reports. Of his wife, he says only that she was "much occupied" in India "writing her important work" on Dante. The couple's time at Kodaikanal was "characterized by some interesting and, indeed, exciting events," he says: "A great spot in September, 1909" and a "great sun-grazing comet" on the morning of January 17, 1910.

John's doctor considered him an "impossible patient" during the final years of his life: "However ill, [he] would always refuse to leave his underground observatory. I well remember having to examine his chest while he was engaged in taking photos of the sun."

Just before her death, Mary received a visit from Barbara Reynolds, a teacher and scholar at Cambridge who had, by chance, run across *Dante and the Early Astronomers* in the Cambridge library. "From then on, I was able to explain the astronomical references to my students instead of saying, as T. S. Eliot did, that they don't matter and you can skip them," Reynolds says. A. D. Thackeray, Mary's nephew, then teaching astronomy at Cambridge Observatory, met Reynolds and arranged an afternoon with Mary. Though Mary was ill, the women spent a pleasant day sharing their love of Florence and Dante's imagery.

At the time, Dorothy L. Sayers was translating *The Divine Comedy* into English. Dante was a "sealed book" to her countrymen, who were raised on "science and psychiatry and television" and therefore "incredibly lacking in literary background," she said. Reynolds introduced her to Mary's "remarkable" book, which Sayers found to be "quite the best guide available to Ptolemaic astronomy and to Dante's handling of celestial phenomena." When Sayers died in 1957, Reynolds completed the translation. She also arranged to reprint Mary's book with Allan Wingate, a London publisher. The second edition met the opposite fate of the first: students of science ignored it but Dantists welcomed its unique approach to the poem. Writing in the *Modern Language Review*, Colin Hardie of Oxford said the book had been "unjustly neglected." He marveled at how "well equipped" Mary was to bring poetry and science to the "general public" as well as to "specialists." In her introduction to the new edition, Reynolds noted that Mary's work "belongs to the period of the amateur-scholar," a "phase of culture" long past.

Generally, now, Dante's astronomy has sunk once more into obscurity, receiving cursory treatment in academic publications—though the poet continues to be appreciated for the accuracy of his science. In 1979 Mark A. Peterson, a physicist at Amherst College, wrote in the *American Journal of Physics* that Dante's conception of the universe in canto 28 of *Paradiso* is "unbelievably apt and accurate" in positing a "three dimensional sphere" with "finite volume" but "no boundary." Dante's genius is to make "verbal arguments which closely parallel . . . mathematics."

In 2000 Alison Cornish, a teacher of Italian, published *Reading Dante's Stars* (Yale University Press), the most extensive study of Dante's celestial imagery since Mary's book. For Cornish, the outstanding feature of Dante's universe is its sensuality, the fact that, according to Dante, God is the "love" that "governs heaven." At the heart of existence is the eroticism of the stars, the dynamics of desire. Mary Ackworth Evershed was the first to tie this aspect of Dante's writing to scientific truths. On a hilltop with her husband, and several hundred pounds of astronomical equipment, she celebrated poetry and the romance of the stars with the unbridled passion of the amateur.

# Silent Screams

Kierkegaard has a secret. In an 1843 journal entry he wrote, "After my death no one will find in my papers the slightest information about what has really filled my life; no one will find ... the rupture ... in my innermost being that interprets everything." He suggested that, without this key, his literary output could not be understood. There is no way to read Kierkegaard. We can only *misread* him.

Yet the readers he draws seize on him with a fervent, almost personal, passion. "Kierkegaard knew very clearly how matters stood," Franz Kafka wrote in his diary in 1913. "He is on my side of the world. He bears me out like a friend."

According to critic Mark C. Taylor, Edvard Munch's painting *The Scream* is a visual representation of the emotional core in Kierkegaard's work. Though Munch finished the painting before he read Kierkegaard, Munch later affirmed he found "remarkable parallels" between himself and the philosopher. In *The Scream*, a tortured figure stands on a wooden bridge, emitting a noise nearby strollers fail to hear. It is beyond their normal understanding. The figure's trouble remains obscure—not because he hasn't let it out, but because he has let it out in a way that others cannot register.

What *is* this silent scream in Kierkegaard that tugged at Kafka and Munch? What connects their literary imaginations?

Based on Kierkegaard's journals, scholars have long speculated that his hidden wound had something to do with his father. As a youth, Michael Kierkegaard blasphemed God, an act he later blamed for casting a curse on his family. All of his children, save Søren and his older brother, died quite young, as did Michael's first wife. These tragedies

compounded his already gloomy temperament and led him to raise
Søren in a harsh, overprotective manner with strict Christian discipline. Søren developed a depressive view of life. For a while, as a young
man, he broke with his father.

Paternal battles consumed Kafka as well. A letter, found in his papers
after his death, begins, "Dearest Father, You asked me recently why I
mention that I am afraid of you. As usual, I was unable to think of any
answer to your question, partly for the very reason that I am afraid of
you.... And if I try to give you an answer in writing, it will still be very
incomplete." He never sent the letter.

In a little blue notebook, Kafka scrawled a series of aphorisms
based on his reading of *Fear and Trembling*, Kierkegaard's meditation
on the ultimate father–son conflict, the one between Abraham and
Isaac. Kierkegaard ponders Abraham's inability to explain his secret—
his willingness to sacrifice his son for the Lord. Kafka concludes that
Abraham suffers from an arrogant "spiritual poverty." He puts himself
above the common run of men. His real problem, Kafka insists, is his
"insufficiently profound mingling with the ... world."

In the unsent letter, Kafka says his father is a "veiled" man, not even
pretending to be engaged with his family or the world around him.

Did these remote and frightening fathers, Kierkegaard's and Kafka's,
sacrifice their sons' mental health while striving for religious and social
propriety? Kierkegaard certainly believed *his* family story ran this way.
Though he reconciled with his father shortly before the older man died,
his resentment lingered. In his journals he complains that his was not
a proper childhood.

Mark Taylor argues that Munch's kinship with Kierkegaard and
Kafka rests in Oedipal terror. *The Scream's* inception lies in an earlier
painting by Munch, *The Dead Mother and Her Child*. A boy, standing
beside his mother's deathbed, opens his mouth to scream. "If we read
*The Scream* in terms of the sketches from which it came and the paintings to which it led, we discover a fascinating chain of signs," Taylor
says. "Despair ... The Scream ... Anxiety ... The Dead Mother." Anxiety,
Taylor reminds us, appears in Kierkegaard's *The Sickness unto Death*
as the "way in which every individual experiences the primordial guilt
associated with original sin."

Kierkegaard seems to have experienced "original sin" in an unusually personal manner. In his home, birth and iniquity were inextricable. His mother was the family's house servant, a woman impregnated by his father shortly after the death of Michael's wife. As a result of this "fall," Michael Kierkegaard withdrew from society. He hurled himself into strenuous religious study and sacrificed any chance Søren might have had for a normal upbringing. Not once in his writing does Kierkegaard mention his mother.

Donald Barthelme (whose best-known novel, a retelling of Oedipal myths, is entitled *The Dead Father*) once said that "by bypassing" a subject in writing, the way Kierkegaard bypassed his mother, "you are able to present it in a much stronger way than if you confronted it directly. I mean there are some things that have to be done by backing into them. . . . [I]ndirection is a way of presenting the thing that somehow works more strongly" to sharpen the emotion.

In the father's shadow, much remains hidden. Silent screams. Absent mothers. Wittgenstein, an avid reader of Kierkegaard, said that, as soon as we name our love, we have spoiled it by exposing it to the world's harshness, blunt as a father's rage.

In a similar spirit, the psychologist Hubert Benoit says a child who has, rightly or wrongly, felt itself "despised" in the Oedipal crush will approach love and Eros indirectly, in fear.

Perhaps it's no surprise, then, that the narratives we encounter in Kierkegaard and Kafka proceed surreptitiously, or that each new literary generation produces a certain number of secretive men with similar imaginations. Oedipal terror appears to haunt the corridors of our culture—its politics as well as its literature. Think of the Kennedy dynasty or the Bush family, the consequences of the conflicts between fathers and sons for women, war, national pride.

As Donald Barthelme writes, in a love story called "Rebecca," "Do I want to be loved *in spite of* [my flaws]? Do you? Does anyone? But aren't we all, to some degree?" Even presidents.

In a whisper, Barthelme's narrator concludes, "[This] story . . . was written for several reasons. Nine of them are secrets."

# Mr. Either and Mr. Or

In France, in the late eighteenth century, a now little-known literary genre flourished that combined the erotic novel and the architectural treatise. *The Little House: An Architectural Seduction* by Jean-François de Bastide is a surviving example of the form. In it, a well-known libertine, the Marquis de Tremicour, "a man of wit and taste . . . unrivaled in his charm," sets out to seduce Mélite, a flirtatious but virtuous young woman. She is "uninhibited," "airy," and possessed of a "certain abandon" around men. Though she rebuffs the marquis's advances, she accepts an invitation to his *petite maison*, a suburban retreat "artfully contrived for love." "Let us follow her there," the narrator tells the reader. We are ushered into "symmetrically arranged yards" supporting "wild and domesticated animals," and into gardens whose foliage offers ingenious glimpses of orchards: a scenic peep show, a prolonged tease, like the narrator's slow and deliberate release of information. Penetration of the house is delayed in a leisurely prologue, five or six pages of literary foreplay.

Once we *are* inside, we follow the couple from parlor to parlor, each room increasing our desire to see the next, exactly as a well-made storyline kindles our curiosity. Sculpted faces adorn doorways and façades. The smell of fruit sweetens the air. The place's textures and furnishings, its alcoves, vestibules, indoor pools, and arcades (all fashioned in clear phallic shapes) sweep Mélite into a sensual paradise, far removed from the world's sorrows.

In every scene, at the height of narrative/erotic energy, *fiction interruptus* occurs, and a formal, didactic voice breaks into the text—the architecture professor drawing our attention to the precise dimensions of a boudoir or to the fabrics used to upholster a divan.

At one point, Mélite, overcome by the beauty of the house, swoons. "Your despair is my delight," purrs the rake. Just as we think he's going to pounce—naked flesh reflected in a series of mirrors on the walls—the narrator announces, "Small but perfectly proportioned," the room "spoke well of the architect's taste. . . . The salon was circular in shape, capped with a dome painted by Hallé," to which a footnote adds, "[Hallé was] one of our French painters, who, along with Boucher, was preeminent in the representation of fables." It's as though Emma Bovary, flushed with carnal heat, had suddenly wandered into a design seminar.

These days, we're well aware of formal properties and formal distinctions in literature. Writers search for the perfect congruence of content and form. To our ears, de Bastide's *The Little House* is an awkward, unworkable mix of fiction and nonfiction. On principle, we're suspicious of patchwork jobs like this. We suspect the book's readers, back in 1760 or so, were trying to get their jollies in secret: "I'm not really interested in the sex. I just want to build a courtyard like the one on page 10."

A bit of historical context. *Petites maisons* were common in eighteenth-century France. Everyone knew about them, but few people spoke of them in polite, middle-class society. Their purpose was to provide a discrete refuge for scandalous play—an intent that also characterized certain novels, perhaps *most* novels, of the period. De Laclos's *Les Liaisons Dangereuses*, published in 1782, is a still-popular example of the era's cheerful literary impurity: moral fables bumping up against erotica, narratives masquerading as journals, letters, diaries. Private made public; education distilled into entertainment; the erotic gone sermonic.

These multiple layers and disguises, smugglings of one intention into another, reveal the novel's uneasiness with itself, its wild ambitions and embarrassed uncertainties. In the eighteenth century the novel was a form without a blueprint. Conversely, textbook and sermon writers, compilers of books of manners, were not opposed to smudging *their* forms a little, if that meant wider dissemination of their aims. Fiction/nonfiction? Either/or? Both? In any case, in certain very polite circles, reading remained a scandalous activity, best pursued in a hidden house, among the dishabille of tossed-off stockings, corsets, ties.

Let's switch rooms. Imagine, for a moment, that we've stepped into a fusty old antique shop with groaning oak floors. Surrounded by free-standing black porcelain sinks, violet drapes, Persian rugs, and other souvenirs salvaged from the lobbies of chi-chi escort services, we've come upon a basket of photographs, torn, yellowing, some of them stuck together, the images peeling: nude women reclining on sofas beneath framed Hallé prints, or standing before a painted desert backdrop.

But you object.

In an antique shop, you say, we're more likely to find pictures of well-dressed men, family portraits, children posing for their parents, and you're right—in any imaginative construct, fiction or nonfiction, verisimilitude is our first requirement. But for the sake of argument, let's assume this shop specializes in remnants of recent—say, early twentieth century—*petite maisons*. Pleasantly erotic photographs are not out of place here.

Further, let's agree that, broadly speaking, there are two kinds of people: one will pluck from the basket a picture of a curly-haired brunette posed before the painted desert and wonder about her story. Who was she, why did she model in this fashion, who stood behind the camera, why a desert?

The other sort of person will dispense with questions and *make up* a story about the woman: perhaps she was an actress, engaged in a prolonged affair with the photographer, a poor young man from Nevada who had made his way to Paris aboard a bedraggled steamer.

Now let's assume that our two browsers, Mr. Either and Mr. Or, are both writers. Mr. Either might pursue the photograph's origins. How did it arrive in this shop, where did it come from, what might that tell us about the woman's time and place; what does the style of the painting reveal; can we determine the nature of the material on which the image appears—canvas, fabric, wood—and will that lead us to a particular region where such material might be purchased or made? Out of his speculations and pursuit, a narrative emerges.

Meanwhile, Mr. Or might use the woman's wry expression as the central image in a fabricated tale about art and love, or the desert might trigger a story set elsewhere, a travel adventure featuring the woman and her lover. *The man whisks her back to Nevada, where, in an unexpected turn of events . . .*

Does anything besides the writer's individual temperament determine whether this photograph lends itself most powerfully to fiction or nonfiction? Both writers begin with the same material, similar knowledge.

The answer to our question, if there *is* a firm answer, would seem to lie in the material itself. So let's examine the photograph more closely. Concentrate on the desert. It appears that the person who painted this backdrop worships Ansel Adams, the famous photographer of the American West, for the landscape depicted is a crude representation of a well-known Adams shot: the rippling, daylighted sand of Hornitos, California, near the California–Nevada border. A white-picket fence spikes up out of the sand. Sunset shoots through the slats of the fence, its afterglow becoming a series of brilliant white doodles on the ground.

Now, let's take a further step back and ponder *Adams's* picture, the one on which the painting is based. The picture's composition—precise, symmetrical, emphasizing stillness—reveals the artist's intention. It's a fiction, of course, to think we can know Adams's intention, but it seems reasonably clear that he wanted to capture the desert's natural appeal. If beauty, or at least a traditional *kind* of beauty, had not been his goal, the layout would be off-kilter, the focus diffuse. The composition would contain elements, or impart an approach, signaling a different ambition.

For many Americans, Adams's work has defined "nature photography." He has had a wide influence on other artists. In the 1980s and 1990s a photographer named Carole Gallagher, mindful of Adams's achievements, traveled across the American West, documenting deserts. Her pictures convey a rangy splendor—majestic skies, a rugged hill, a quaint house in which lovers might embrace. Consciously, Gallagher echoes Adams's images. In one picture, a wire barrier bisects puckered sand like the fence in Hornitos. The scene is pretty and serene. Then we read the photo's caption. Events take an unexpected turn: "Animal cages near ground zero, Frenchman Flat, 1990."

In *American Ground Zero: The Secret Nuclear War*, Gallagher explains that "during the atmospheric testing era, atomic veterans testify that they saw both animals and humans chained in cages close to ground zero." Look again. Gallagher's composition no longer pleases the eye. Objectively, its appearance hasn't changed. It is still pretty and serene, but the artist's intention has altered it for us. Uncertainty becomes the aesthetic principle organizing our response. If lovers are clinging inside the house—which is also, it turns out, a target on Frenchman Flat—they huddle in pain.

For us, Adams's portraits will never again shimmer with innocence. Gallagher has composed a bold coda to his project, a respectful but scalding critique.

Sometimes, in order to heighten nature's purity, Ansel Adams airbrushed people out of his pictures. Often, the loveliness in his photos is a fiction, just as the beauty in Gallagher's shots hides awful truths.

In encountering works of art, our reaction is guided by what we perceive, rightly or wrongly, to be the artist's intention—and this occurs *despite the material.* The fence may exemplify symmetry or cruelty. The house may accommodate seduction or doom.

Often, in the act of composition—the *encounter with material*—an artist will blur her motives, intentionally or unintentionally (or she may not know *what* she wants to do with her triggering subject). Naturally, in the process, literary categories may also blur.

Some of the smudgiest blurs in Western literature can be found in the work of Marcel Proust. For instance, in *Swann's Way*, he describes a man waking, startled and tense, like this: "When a man is asleep, he has in a circle round him the chain of the hours, the sequence of the years. Instinctively, when he awakes, he looks to these, and in an instant reads off his own position on the earth's surface."

Here's what interests me about Proust's passage: if we didn't know these lines came from a novel, could we identify them as part of a work of fiction? Can we tell the difference between actual observation and pure imagination?

Obviously not. Or at least not always. Context—intent—is all.

But if *our* intent is either/or—that is, to separate fiction and nonfiction—it's worth asking the following question (bear with me, because the question is almost impossible to articulate): can life-experiences, objects and events, communicate intentionality, guiding us toward one shape or another as we try to fix their presences?

In other words—and this is where we started—does our material tell us what to do with it?

Common sense wants to turn this question around. It seems logical to say *we* impose *our* intentions on experiences, perceiving objects and events through personal biases, limitations, and preconceptions, arranging them to fit our needs.

But common sense is the enemy of seduction.

Quickly—do you remember the last time you swooned?

Like Mélite, I've been enraptured by pretty sights, sounds, and smells. Braids of sand, the weave of a rock-face, or tunes in windy trees can overtake me before I've recovered enough to hide my animal response. Shamed by my high emotions—am I crazy or, even worse, sentimental, my God did anyone see me pause just now, my mouth stupidly open, what will people think of me?—I arrange an appropriate mask to cover my embarrassment: an analysis, an ironic quip, a distancing remark. Propriety is preserved.

What I'm trying to say is this: possibly, the shapes of longing are tucked inside of things, and speak to us about what to do with them—and our response is immediate, visceral, though we may (and usually do) *overthink* that response to preserve decorum.

Perhaps the earthwork art of the 1960s and 1970s best illustrates what I'm fumbling for: Walter de Maria's *Lightning Field* in a New Mexico desert, demonstrating the planet's perspicacity in pulling electricity out of the air, or Robert Smithson's *Spiral Jetty* in Utah, revealing the planet's patient dance—the life of what we commonly feel to be lifeless.

Giacometti once insisted that, while staring at a stone, he could see in its contours the shape a potential sculpture would take. It was not only that he could *imagine* fashioning a piece from the rock. No. Something deeper than that. The sculpture, he claimed, already existed *within* the rock, and his job was simply to free it.

I'm aware that this sort of talk doesn't help the writer struggling with craft, whose questions are more immediate: does a particular experience have enough dramatic arc to support a fictional framework, or do its outlines require a more discursive approach? Is the power of this experience in the fact that it actually happened? Do I know enough about this subject? If not, why not make something up? Is it ethical for me to appropriate this material for imaginative ends or does propriety dictate a more straightforward presentation?

But I would argue that these immediate problems are shaped by a deeper concern. For lack of a better term, I'll call it "the spiritual." The spiritual is largely out of place in the world of seduction—we *did* begin with seduction!—which often depends on deceitful manipulation of the environment.

But perhaps it's not *always* out of place.

Consider, again, *petites maisons*. The designers of these houses agreed with their literary contemporaries, writers like Diderot and Voltaire, that a disposition for aesthetic appreciation was a natural faculty. *Le sens interne du beau*: a bodily ability to apprehend spiritual beauty and to separate truth from fiction. Diderot believed this disposition was located in some physical organ we couldn't detect. Its purpose, he said, was to "discover quickly and keenly the degree of pleasure that each thing should afford us."

The builders of Little Houses tweaked this pleasure-sense and gilded their spaces with sexy distractions, erasing all thoughts of history, routine, aging, and death. Just as walls, painted with "odorless paint," shield pipes and wires, and paper covers plaster, the seducer obfuscates as much as he communicates. His words, like his rooms, are made to conceal.

Which brings us finally to the center of my own little structure here—to what, if anything, this essay has to offer that is new about literary form. I believe we use form to *conceal* as well as to reveal our primary subjects (as matter conceals spirit), and concealment gives our

subjects their power. The glimpse is far more seductive than the prolonged stare.

Fiction or nonfiction—it doesn't much matter. Or at least, the question should not detain us. What we need to be clear about, so we can
*form* our stories with the utmost skill, is the fact that we shape material to mask our desires and shame: shame at our animal natures, our
sentimentality, and our vague spiritual yearnings. After all, in Western
culture, literature is a middle-class form, and the middle classes are riddled with fear of scandal, fear of mute objects (their capacity to *outlive*
us), fear of the sensual world. Form, then, as odorless paint. A tasteful
veneer.

*Either/Or* was the title of Søren Kierkegaard's first major book, and it's
appropriate to turn to him now, for no writer has played with literary
forms more engagingly than Kierkegaard. He is perhaps history's greatest anti-libertine. The polite society of Copenhagen, where he lived in
the early to mid-nineteenth century, tolerated no romantic scandals,
so when he broke his engagement to Regine Olsen, a young woman
from a fine family, he was privately and publicly scorned. By then,
Kierkegaard had already published *Either/Or*. He had come to feel he
had a higher calling than marriage—namely, to be God's witness to the
truth at a time when official institutions, patently corrupt, glutted legal
documents and daily newspapers with self-serving fictions.

Shortly after the break with Regine, but while he considered a rec-
onciliation with her, he published *Fear and Trembling*. As we saw in the
previous essay, ostensibly the book was an examination of Abraham's
faith (from Genesis 22). It arrived in shops under a pseudonym,
Johannes de Silencio. The name springs from a Grimm's fairy tale about
a king's servant named Johannes who remains mum about his doings
to protect his master and a princess.

*Fear and Trembling* has a fairy tale beginning: "Once upon a time
there was a man [Johannes] who had learned as a child that beautiful
tale of how God tried Abraham." As the story proceeds, readers familiar with Kierkegaard's romantic troubles begin to see a book within a
book. "No reflection can bring about a movement" in life, Johannes says.
"This requires passion," but sadly, Johannes is a reflective man, obsessed

with common sense and proper form—with tamping down his passions. In reflecting on Abraham's contradictory impulses—whether or not to obey God's command—Johannes is left with a "darkened eye. He saw joy no more."

Is Kierkegaard writing these lines to Regine, a disguised apology for his contradictory feelings for her? A roundabout explanation of his desertion? A seduction? The answer to these questions appears to be yes, especially when he describes Abraham's decision to sacrifice his boy. Kierkegaard uses the analogy of a romance: Abraham's act resembles a knight's acceptance of his duty to a greater good. It means passing up his princess.

Why does Kierkegaard mask himself so elaborately here?

Once again, Proust may offer some insight. In his day, he faced problems eerily similar to Kierkegaard's. "Our social personality is a creation of the thoughts of other people," Proust says early in *Swann's Way*. "We pack the physical outline of [a] person we see with all the notions we have already formed about him, and in ... the end [these notions] come to fill out so completely the curve of his cheeks, to follow so exactly the line of his nose ... that each time we see the face ... it is these notions which we recognise and to which we listen." In other words, to each other we are flesh-and-blood fictions.

What was true of Proust's Paris was doubly true of Kierkegaard's Copenhagen. Aware of his "social personality," as fixed by newspaper gossip following his botched engagement, Kierkegaard tucked his truth inside a fiction within a fiction within a meditation, to speak to the soul of his love, preserving taste, concealing his shame, and most importantly, keeping what mattered to him sacrosanct. As Hamlet, that prince of indirection, insists, "Whatever shall hap[pen] ... give it understanding, but no tongue."

In this difficult process, Kierkegaard has, of course, admitted and preserved his shame for those who read carefully, and who feel a kinship with his agonies and doubts. Form provides a space, across distance and time, where intimacy between author and reader can grow.

Ultimately, the question in all of Kierkegaard's writing is this, and it has everything to do with *form*: to what degree, and in what manner, do we wish to be bound by what we say? It is a question he asks of himself (a man who broke his promise), a challenge posed to his fellows, to God, and to every object on earth. It is a question probing the boundaries of human consciousness and its connection to the things around it.

Proust again: "When I saw any external object, my consciousness that I was seeing it would remain between me and it, enclosing it in a slender, incorporeal outline which prevented me from ever coming directly in contact with the material form." Without direct contact—or the words to forge a form to grip our minds—what responsibilities do we have to anything around us? How crippled are we by our failure to *listen to* things, to comprehend how our failure affects the environments we create (*petites maisons, ground zero, animal cages*)?

A side note (a small parlor, as it were, just off the main corridor of our discussion): Kierkegaard was deeply suspicious of science, but it's an irony he might have appreciated that Werner Heisenberg developed the Uncertainty Principle in Copenhagen. "Method [i.e. form] and object cannot be separated," Heisenberg wrote in 1927, a still-current claim that could have leaped from Kierkegaard's journals more than half a century earlier. It means we can't really study the world. We can only study our study of it.

To end *this* particular study, let's return to the fiction/nonfiction conundrum, and do so indirectly, by way of a parable. After all, we should never stop playing with form.

"Exotic Masks—Comedy, Tragedy!" says a sign in a grimy shop window on a narrow city street. "Revealing Photographs! Precious Trinkets! Imported from Copenhagen, Paris, Hornitos!" Mr. Either, arm-in-arm with Mr. Or, steps from the shop's doorway, ringing a tiny bell.

Suddenly, a reckless carriage takes a corner, nearly crushing a man in the street. Precipitously, an arm pulls the man from the path of the horses (a pair of handsome mares the color of desert sand). The arm belongs to a lanky marquis, a well-known libertine. He straightens the man's coat—a shameful rag, a parody of a coat—pats his crooked shoulder, asks if he's well, then, recognizing him as a notable thinker, politely asks about his latest publication. *Fear and Something? Fear and Scandal? Fear and the Modern Novel?* Wonderful writing. Elegant, thoughtful, but rather obscure, don't you agree, impractical, pie-in-the-sky, fiction, "truth" and such.

Yes, well, says the man in the ragged coat, plainly agitated at being detained by this unsavory fellow. He hopes there are no reporters, no gossip mongers, about. He had wanted to be alone, to walk, to be lost in the rhythms of his imagination. Nervously, he prattles to the marquis about God and faith, life's highest callings. Across the way, just outside an architect's window full of colorful blueprints ("Suburban House—Hidden Retreat"), a young woman twirls a yellow parasol, a wry abandon apparent in the tilt of her head. Though the libertine is no longer listening, the thinker, transfixed by the girl, admits in a trembling whisper, *"And yet it must be wonderful to get the princess."*

# A Pigeon Coop, a Crystal Palace

When I was growing up, my mother and my sister, four years younger than I, fought at the supper table each night: food, clothes, homework, boys, and drugs, you name it. My father sat at one end of the table, opposite me, and between us, these girls we loved tore into each other.

My mother dismissed my sister's choices. *You have to finish your pork chops, you're way too thin. I'm telling you: don't go near Sam Weaver, he'll have you knocked up and boiling wieners in a trailer home.*

My sister protested. *I can't eat this; your greasy old food puts pimples on my chin. Yeah, Sam's kind of a doofus, but he's teaching me the chords to "Stairway to Heaven."*

They never threw dishes or silverware, though often, rising to make a point, my sister kicked her chair. After ice cream, I'd flee the table for the quiet of our backyard. The West Texas nights were always warm. The boy next door, four or five years older than I was, raised pigeons. When he first got the birds, he kept them caged behind nets of loose wire mesh, scattered without any structural supports in the middle of the yard. He'd attach a bubble of mesh to the lawn with plastic tent spikes. Slowly, over the course of one summer, he put together a rectangular wooden frame and nailed the mesh to it. The more elaborate the coop became, the shabbier it looked, but at least the pigeons had room now to flap about and scrabble in the dirt. Some of them made brief flights around the pen then hugged the ground as though exhausted from having traveled round the world. I loved listening to the birds. Their hubbub distracted me from the shouting inside our house.

I took to sitting in the evenings on the long brick wall out back. I'd watch the pigeons and read a book, trying to ignore my family's turmoil. Dusk brushed the sky, purple and orange. From my perch, I could see my neighbor's fences, spray-painted with graffiti: "Stu loves Stephie," "Billy sucks."

Mostly, the books I read had been assigned to me by my schoolteachers: Homer, Hemingway, novels, stories, fables. Eventually, encouraged by one of my English instructors, a fellow who moonlighted as a DJ on a local rock 'n' roll radio station and who, late at night, analyzed Patti Smith lyrics on the air, I turned to Dostoevsky and Beckett. I dipped into Kierkegaard—not for any class credit, but simply to learn: a novel concept. As the sun set each day in a haze of Texas dust, philosophy and fiction began to mix for me, just as the cooing of the pigeons slipped into my sister's sobbing.

I thought surely, once Sis came of age, she would skip town the first chance she got. Instead, I'm the one who left home in his twenties, moved half a country away, out of the tumbleweed desert, to an environment more conducive to reading and writing.

My sister stayed in the old neighborhood. For years, she lived just up the block from my mother. She'd bring laundry down to be washed. She'd ask Mom to babysit her boy. I came to see that the old fury between them sprang from the fact that they understood they were exactly alike.

"No ideas but in things," said William Carlos Williams, implying, as succinctly as a line of graffiti, the primary tension between philosophy and fiction: the assumption that philosophy soars while fiction scrabbles in the soil. Philosophy speculates on possibility, fidgets with the invisible, while fiction circles whatever's in front of it, leaving its messy tracks on the world.

Some of this I learned, sitting on the wall. For instance, I grasped that fiction longs for drama. Drama depends on gravity and the body, the body's beauty and bulk, its susceptibility to pain. Fiction is suited to narrative pratfalls.

Conversely, philosophy longs for symmetry and sweet perfection, transcendence, all of which leave the body behind.

And yet, as William Gass says, seen solely as a plot device, what could be more dramatic than *spirit* knocked loose from the *body*? Death: a flight into the ether. It makes an incredible story, and it belongs to speculative philosophy. Infinity, The Fates, Lady Fortune, God—philosophy's cast of characters is dazzling. On balance, it dwarfs fiction's giants. Melville's wimpy old whale? Please!

Still, everyone knows God's a bore. Just ask Milton. Fiction's itchy kids, Huck Finn, Little Nell, talk circles around the Almighty. They're not afraid to shout their names at the sky or leave funny doodles in the dirt.

No ideas but in things.

Williams's formulation argues a difference. But it notes a curious kinship, as well. Perhaps a mutual fear separates *things* and *ideas*. Philosophy frets: if it gets too cozy on the ground, it will lose its urge to fly. Fiction fears the air, the thin, cool atmosphere: drama requires an excess of heavy breathing.

Each night after supper, sitting on that stony West Texas wall, struggling to understand Kierkegaard and Beckett, I recognized astonishing parallels between philosopher and novelist, or at least *this* philosopher, *this* novelist. To begin with, both stressed the importance of the immediate moment. Maybe, I thought, fiction and philosophy weren't so far apart, after all.

For the sake of argument, then, let's scratch the notion that fiction captures the world while philosophy touches whatever roils unseen behind it. After all, fiction has never agreed with itself, one writer to the next, on what the world really looks like. Victor Hugo would never have recognized or remotely condoned Hemingway's Paris.

And philosophy is quite capable of holding a polished mirror to the Here and Now.

Let's be clear. Fiction doesn't represent *anything*. It makes things with words. Philosophy doesn't theorize *anything*. It rearranges language. Like mother and daughter, they're separate but alike.

"You read too much," my dear old father used to tell me. On the weekends, when my sister was away from the house, eating pizza with her friends or learning guitar chords from her sometime-boyfriend, my father would knock on my bedroom door. "Look at you," he'd say. "You're not doing anyone a lick of good, sitting here with your face in a book."

"Uh-huh," I'd say, turning a page. On the particular Saturday I have in mind now, I'd been reading a volume I'd found at a neighbors' garage sale, a paperback about the Crystal Palace, the famous exhibition space built in London in the early 1850s. The palace was a steel and glass museum housing the Western nations' latest designs in furniture, industry, and the arts, in machinery and weapons.

"Are you listening to me?" my father said. "Oughta get outside, mow the lawn. I'm *talking* to you! I swear, son, where's your head?"

After weeding and mowing the backyard, I clambered up the wall and watched the boy next door feed his birds. He was chubby and short. He wore Levis every day, and the same red T-shirt. Running or even walking he looked awkward, jerky and uncoordinated, but sometimes as he circled his pigeon coop, sifting yellow feed through his fingers, attending the needs of his flock, his body acquired a patient, lovely grace.

"Hey," I called to him that Saturday afternoon.

"Hey," he said.

"How many birds you got?"

"Nine."

"Nice coop."

"I guess."

I suppose I was overheated by the Crystal Palace, dreaming of airy pavilions, because I remember saying to him, "You know what? I'll bet if you added a little glass on the sides there, and some metal strips in the corners, you could really *make* something of this coop."

Apparently ignoring me, he stuffed loose feathers into a plastic trash bag.

The world awaited a spectacular future: that's what I'd gleaned from the palace catalogue. The catalogue said tomorrow's ideals were embodied *today* in the pistons, rifles, chairs, and urns on display inside the lovely structure. The palace, I imagined, was a galleon of spun sugar, breath, and dewy spider webs.

"I have a book," I explained to the boy. "It's about this cool building. It might give you some ideas. You could, I don't know, tie some helium balloons to the top of your coop there, give it some flair, fix it up a little, and maybe even charge people to come see it."

"Yeah, I don't have much time to read," he mumbled. "I've got my chores and stuff." With that, he turned and, in one fluid movement, filled a tin bowl with water from a garden hose.

Like my neighbor's awkward body with its surprising flashes of grace, language contains multiple, sometimes contradictory, qualities; it can range from the concrete to the abstract and anywhere in between. Based on temperament, metabolism, nerve endings, family traits, cultural assumptions, and a host of other factors, different writers will choose to develop different muscles in their work.

To understand philosophy and fiction, separately and in tandem, we need to grasp the choices they make, and note the options they've dropped, while accepting that neither is "the truth." Neither is "the way to live," unless we choose to live in books instead of the world. (I know where my father stood on *that* question.)

In philosophy as well as fiction, we've entered an artificial realm, regardless of the claims individual texts make on our lives. The artificial has a temperament distinct from us. A distinct metabolism. Yet it's also true that the artificial and the actual engage with remarkable vigor.

A brief digression: for twenty years, I lived with my mother and my sister. The unspoken rules that marked their bond (whether or not Mom and Sis were conscious of them) bore no resemblance to the personal codes binding *me* to the family structure. My relationships with my parents were quite different from my sister's, and naturally affected how I felt about *family* and *relationships* in general. If I walked into the kitchen while a mother–daughter fight ensued, I had to suspend my usual notions of compassion. Could their yelling *really* be a form of love (because I *knew* they loved each other)? Could I feel sorry for *both* of them, while at the same time dismissing them as just a little nuts?

In time, the contrast between my ideals (of compassion, rational behavior) and the facts began to instruct me. My views of the possibilities of human experiences and the complexities of love and daily life expanded. Daily life was a lot more varied than I'd thought.

Back to choices.

William Gass writes, "The man who makes a thing that moves utilizes the laws of motion, although he may be unaware of their existence." Likewise, when a novelist creates a verbal world, her subjects, word choices, and syntax suggest laws of motion that the willing reader readily accepts.

These laws can be explicit, as in Edwin Abbey's mathematical fable *Flatland*, where the characters are geometrical figures living in a two-dimensional world, or, as in the case of most literary fiction, implicit, as when Jane Austen's narrator insists that every successful man must be in want of a wife. As an assertion of truth, a guide to getting about in the world, this statement is questionable, but it serves its fiction by establishing the laws of motion, the social customs, the cultural assumptions, the economic and educational backgrounds, the style and form that governs, like gravity, the story being told. It posits the ideals by which we evaluate, through contrast and incongruity, what actually happens in the story—the way *I* figured out, or tried to, my mother and sister in the kitchen.

Forgive me again for interrupting myself, but before going any further, and to help us on the way, allow me to stipulate: the world is undeniably *there*.

This assertion is not as obvious or uncontestable as it might seem. For centuries, certain philosophers and literary theorists have insisted, "Nothing is real except our perceptions."

Nonsense. Let me just say it. Kick a chair. Clutch your throbbing toe and *then* tell me the goddamn chair isn't real.

Granted, it may not be *solid*—a physicist once told me that space exists between the individual atoms within objects and inside our bodies so theoretically it's possible, I suppose, to attack the chair and experience the atoms in your foot sliding past the atoms in the wood. But you're smart enough not to try this and so am I.

So. Let's agree the world is a given. Objects in the world are a given. What is *not* a given is their meaning to us, our intentions for them, or the way our consciousness will choose to engage them.

Phenomenologists such as Edmund Husserl tell us that consciousness *makes* things. Not literally, in the case of the chair—the chair sits here already—but the chair can be made into a place to rest our butts or a surface on which to stack our books, or it can be torn apart, rearranged, and made into a sculpture, or it can be made into a sculpture by virtue of our agreeing to call it one. Depending on what our consciousness intends, this chair contains numerous possibilities. Its actualization here, now, in this form, serving this particular function, is merely one choice among many.

This is a more complex concept of the assertion, "Nothing is real except our perceptions." Our perceptions, what I'm calling *consciousness*, take what's given and remakes it according to our needs, whims, desires. The pigeon coop can be a cage or it can be a crystal palace.

How the birds see it, of course, is another matter.

The philosopher Merleau-Ponty says we embrace the world when the given-ness of objects matches our intentionality for them. When we turn to something, we're aware of being aware of it, and whatever we make of a thing—this chair is an attractive piece of furniture; no, it's fodder for a sculpture; no, it's an example of global production—reveals our intentionality.

Our awareness of objects becomes *self*-awareness. She's an aesthete, you're a polemicist, I'm a natterer and a fool. How do we know? Well— how does each of us see the chair?

Of course, our views can change. I could show you a stone and you could study it, noting its color, shape, and texture. You would decide if it held any significance for you. If I then told you this stone was once part of a building attacked by a terrorist and that it was handed to me by a survivor of the bombing after the building crumbled, the stone's meaning would shift for you.

Further, when we really view a thing, turning upon it our full powers of concentration and imagination, we see not only what it is in its present form and function, but what it has been and what it *might* be. We see its possibilities. Our awareness can re-choose, re-name, re-figure on its behalf. An object truly apprehended is a unity of all its many options, its contingent, temporal form and what it is not, the nothing (the-not-yet-something) within it, waiting to be born. In this way, we invest objects with ideas as well as actuality, with the abstract as well as the concrete, with the possible as well as the inevitable, the infinite as well as the finite. In doing all this work, consciousness measures its reach. It haunts the world as the spirit of what the world might be, what it might yet become.

Like a siren in Homer's *Odyssey*, consciousness calls to us, Don't follow the prevailing winds! Believe me, *this* direction is much more promising—turn your sails over here, over here, no, over there.

Which brings us back to fiction. What is fiction but an invitation to consider the unreal as a way of sussing the real, to examine possibility for a clearer grasp of the actual, to consider ideas as a way of seeing things?

This is fiction's strategy: what if *this* happened, it asks, or *that*? We can seize this chair and re-make it.

Fiction seizes *us*, and in some form or another, the object of *its* contemplation, *its* intentionality, is human nature, human experience. Fiction constructs a site of possible meaning, sometimes shabby, held together with wire, sometimes ethereal, in which the familiar becomes unfixed, newly considered, re-rendered. A writer's fiction, the choices she makes and drops, reveals the shapes of her consciousness. In conforming to or rejecting a particular fictional rendering, a reader's consciousness defines itself.

One last point along these lines: a work of fiction is an object in the world, like a chair. A work of philosophy is an object in the world. Neither fiction nor philosophy does the world much good, at least not directly. But they give consciousness something to play with, to strengthen its motor skills. This is the family business, the source of spats between the two, but also of all their enduring bonds.

Another digression—useful, I hope. When he was growing up, Kierkegaard was keenly aware of the turmoil in his father's house: no knockabouts or shouts, but a quiet rage within his dad between religious ideals and the shameful realities of daily life. The house was curtained and dark. As I noted in the previous essays, Kierkegaard's father was severe with him, but the two of them shared an evening ritual that Kierkegaard cherished all his life. His father would say, "Let's take a walk around the city." They wouldn't leave the house. Instead, they'd imagine the streets. Kierkegaard's father insisted on getting every name, every detail right—the color of a window shutter, the smell of an alley, the sounds of the birds, the script on a shop sign—all remembered from actual walks father and son had taken once. On these evenings, they traveled the real city, their *given*, but the travel was speculative, an experience giving Kierkegaard exceptional insights into the natures of imagination and consciousness, and the bonds between philosophy and fiction.

His books are hard to classify. For example, *Fear and Trembling*, published in 1843, purports to be a philosophical tract on the concept of faith. It offers two contrasting examples of faithful men: Abraham, charged by God to kill his son; and a figure called the Knight of Faith, who looks and acts like an ordinary citizen—a tax collector or a shop owner. Abraham's situation places him beyond ethical bounds. To prove his faith in God, he must commit a heinous act. He must place his individual necessities and his personal sacrifice above universal laws of comportment. He must summon extraordinary courage. By contrast, the Knight of Faith lives entirely within the framework of commonly accepted behavior. His individuality is unremarkable; he is a good if bland husband, a loyal worker, a friend. The incompatibility of these two models makes *Fear and Trembling* an unusual if not utterly confounding philosophical argument. What is Kierkegaard's purpose here?

The book appeared under the pseudonym Johannes de Silencio. Kierkegaard created a false memoirist to tell the story of his search for faith. "When I think about Abraham I am virtually annihilated," says de Silencio. "I am all the time aware of that monstrous paradox that is the content of Abraham's life, and my thought for all its passion is unable to enter into it. To kill one's child to prove one's faith in

God—it's a grotesque absurdity. The traditional literary hero perform-ing great feats for the good of his fellows I can think myself into, but not Abraham. I cannot close my eyes and hurl myself trustingly into the absurd. For me it is impossible."

Miserably, he concludes, "I do not have faith. This courage I lack."

In the wake of his spiritual defeat, he considers the Knight of Faith. I can't be Abraham, I can't climb the mountain, he thinks; so, is it pos-sible I can live an ordinary life here in the city and still be a true man of faith? To find out, de Silencio ponders his daily experience. But even here, his thinking fails. The essence of faith eludes him. "I can very well imagine the Knight of Faith," he begins optimistically. "I come a little closer to him, watch the least movement in case some small message from the infinite should appear, a glance, expression, gesture, a sadness, a smile, betraying the infinite by its incongruity with the finite. But no, look at him. He belongs altogether to the world. This man takes plea-sure, takes part in everything. To see him you would think he's some pen-pusher, who'd lost his soul to book-keeping." De Silencio's anguish grows. "I have tried in vain to spy out the genius of the Knight of Faith," he says. "It could drive me to fury out of envy. The man is perfectly calm, yet he has made, and is at every moment making, the movement of infinity. What is he doing that I can't manage? What is the difference between us?"

At this point in our reading, we note: whatever philosophical flights we may be making here, we are also witnessing *character development*. Our feet are firmly on the ground, right beside Johannes de Silencio (a fictional character). Kierkegaard is not constructing, a la Hegel, a vast logical system to explain the universe. He's offering a drama of one man's struggle for faith. "There was once a man. He had learned as a child that beautiful tale of how God tried Abraham," the story begins. "The older he became, the more his thoughts returned to that tale, and yet less and less could he understand it."

The once-upon-a-times of our childhood, so comforting in our innocence, become maddeningly complex as we age and apply mature reasoning to them. This is de Silencio's torment, and also perhaps the flaw in his being. He was closer to grasping faith as a boy, when he simply enjoyed Abraham's story instead of trying to pry it apart with reason. His dilemma—"I am annihilated"—is poignant because his consciousness will not release him from reasoning. Yet reasoning bars him forever from faith.

For fiction, Kierkegaard's brilliance lies in demonstrating how the torments of thought can be a source of drama; a dialectical, self-questioning structure supplies enormous narrative tension. For philosophy, his importance lies in showing how the plight of one person in daily experience can be fruitful ground for speculation. In Kierkegaard's work, philosophy gives birth to a powerful and ambitious form of fiction.

Twenty years after *Fear and Trembling*, Dostoevsky firmly established the viability of the philosophical novel. *Notes from Underground* (1864) begins, "I am a sick man," echoing a line from Kierkegaard's journals: "I've barely read or thought of a disease before I have it myself."

The novel is a harrowing chronicle of one man's unforgiving self-examination. Dostoevsky does not write under a pseudonym, but he affixes a note at the beginning of the story, distancing himself from his character: "Such persons as the underground man not only may, but must exist in our society, taking into consideration the circumstances under which our society has generally been formed." Like Kierkegaard penning philosophical fragments instead of vast ethical systems, Dostoevsky offers a glimpse to elucidate reasons why a man utterly shut off from his fellows had to appear among us: a tiny drama contrasting Tolstoy's all-encompassing portraits. Dostoevsky parrots romantic poetry and sentimental novels. All of these devices—distancing techniques, fragmented structure, literary parody—alert the reader to the act of reading: consciousness becoming aware of itself.

For writers of fiction, Dostoevsky's novel is a manual for turning abstract concepts into characters, setting, and scene. Part 1 is an extended rant by the narrator; part 2 is a dramatic recreation of everything he has been telling us. Part 1 is speculation—forgive my philosophizing, he says. Part 2 is representation: it shows us how he became the disagreeable polemicist we have just met.

Initially, the underground man moans about awareness. It is torment. "I was conscious every moment of so many elements in myself," he says. "I felt them simply swarming in me, stirred by the variety of choices civilization offers its citizens." Civilization's contradictory paths and his inability to choose among them cause him to qualify every statement he makes: "I lied about myself just now. I'm joking, of course." Very quickly, the reader learns not to trust him.

In part 2, he stops talking so incessantly, at least to us, and we follow him across the city. We go with him to a brothel, where he tells a long story to a young, impressionable prostitute named Liza. The story concerns the dangers of the life she has chosen, and the redemption love can offer. With love, one can live even without happiness, he insists. Life is good even in grief; it's good to live in the world.

By now we know he rarely means a word he says: the scene is thick with irony. More importantly, we have stood in Liza's place—he's lying to *her* the way he lied to *us*. As we watch her falling for him, we want to shout "No!"

A third element enters the scene: his self-delusion. We know from part 1 that his lies are rarely intentionally malicious. Not at first. They're born of his torments; one of his greatest sorrows is his desire, and his inability, to believe his own words.

In the brothel scene, we fear for him as well as for Liza; his untruths will undo them both. Hoping for the love he has promised her, Liza appears one night at his shabby apartment (bitterly, he calls it his palace). He falls into sobbing. He's sorry for lying, for being caught in his lies, for being trapped in tawdriness—most of all, he's sorry for being aware of his awareness. Self-consciousness will not stop torturing him.

At a telling point in his narrative, the underground man mocks himself and us. You believe in a crystal edifice, he sneers, an imaginary structure, beautiful and perfect, in which man can live in happiness and peace. But what good is a crystal palace if, inside it, one still nurtures doubts? Man will always doubt as long as he exists in the world. He will always rip the stones from the buildings he has built. He will never renounce real suffering—destruction and chaos. Suffering is the activity of consciousness.

Just think, he says: if it starts to rain, and a man ducks into a chicken coop to get dry, his gratitude for shelter soon gives way to awareness that he is sitting in a ratty old chicken coop. His suffering starts anew.

Eighty years after *Notes from Underground*, Samuel Beckett took Dostoevsky's concepts of suffering and stripped away the props of setting and scene to emphasize consciousness itself. He located the intentionality at the heart of awareness.

Nothing to be done, says Gogo in *Waiting for Godot* (1948). Sitting around, vainly anticipating some purpose—it's awful. Yet, as Pozzo says, we don't seem to be able to depart, that is, to get out of our chattering heads. When nothing matters and nothing's to be done, consciousness will find something to do anyway, just to keep itself busy. "That's the idea, let's contradict each other," it will pass the time, Gogo tells Didi. It is the drama of intentioning that Beckett's work so movingly presents.

He forces the play's audience to share Didi's and Gogo's frustration that nothing is happening. We wait along with them, then the cycle of waiting repeats, an interminable expectation of . . . well, we don't know any more than the characters do. *Godot* keeps starting over, smothering us in the boredom of routine. Then unexpectedly the play shifts into action, revealing bodies and objects as they are. Stripped of our trained perceptions of them, they stand starkly in all their wonder and terror—the essential, Beckett says. He has not just created a fiction of self-awareness, he's fashioned an *experience* of it. "Charming evening we're having," Didi quips. He may as well be addressing an impatient audience member: I'm sorry you're as self-aware as I am; let me entertain you with a pratfall or two.

Through language, thought becomes ambulatory. Language is the mind's awkward body, tripping all over itself. The passing of time is simulated through the imagining of objects. Metaphor and simile are primary here, and philosophical writing depends on them, heavily: being is breath, self-awareness a vaudeville show.

Roughly around the time Kierkegaard and Dostoevsky wrote their finest works, a literary period that also introduced us to Huck Finn and Little Nell, narrative fiction developed what David Lodge calls free indirect speech. This technique may be fiction's ablest contribution to philosophical speculation. In fiction, we may find a combination of narrative description and quoted speech, as in, "'Is that the clock striking twelve?' Cinderella exclaimed. 'Dear me, I shouldn't be late!'"

There is reported or indirect speech, as in, "Cinderella inquired if the clock was striking twelve, and expressed a fear that she would be late."

Then, there is free indirect speech: "Was that the clock striking twelve? She would be late." In this final example, Lodge says, Cinderella's concern is a silent, private thought, expressed in her own words to which we are given access without the overt mediation of a narrator. The effect is to place the narrative inside Cinderella's consciousness. To say it another way, the third- and first-person points of view *fuse* here, as do the speculative and the representational (to return to the terms I've been using).

In the twentieth century, an increasing awareness of grammatical and narrative techniques led to frequent textual *demonstrations* of consciousness. Beckett's work is perhaps the shining example. But even in more straightforward narratives, stylistic self-consciousness could add a metaphysical underpinning to an apparently simple story. For example, in Ernest Hemingway's "A Clean, Well-Lighted Place" (1933), we see a lack of metaphors and similes, and a dearth of adjectives, forcing the story's objects to emerge in all their raw thing-ness: "The leaves of the tree made shadows against the electric light. The waiter poured on into the glass, so that the brandy slopped over and ran down the stem into the top saucer on the pile."

Many factors contributed to Hemingway's celebrated prose style, but a phenomenological impulse lies behind it—a meditative and obsessive focus on objects stripped of our usual assumptions about them, elevated to a literary aesthetic. John Paul Sartre realized this when he started searching for a form of fiction to embody his philosophical principles. Biographer Ronald Hayman says that Sartre had been seeking since the 1920s a means of blending philosophical reflection with the direct transcription of personal experience. He sought a literary form that would bypass the familiar opposition between realism and idealism, affirming the supremacy of reason as well as the reality of the visible world. Sartre wanted to be able to sit in a sidewalk café, talk about a chair, and call it philosophy.

Hemingway was a revelation for him. Papa made apparently insignificant details significant without relying on subjectivism, says Hayman.

Objects in his narratives were conspicuously solid, though he offered no more than would have been apparent to the character he was creating. This technique, pushed to an extreme, allowed Sartre, in his work, to emphasize both brute being and awareness of being.

Famously, in *Nausea* (1938), Sartre's narrator Roquentin says of a chestnut tree, "Its presence pressed itself against my eyes." Usually, he says, "existence hides itself," but now existence had unveiled its essence to him: "It had lost the harmless look of an abstract category—it was the very paste of things, this tree root was kneaded into existence." Awareness straddles the fence between past and present, present and future. Sartre illustrates this by an excessive use of the colon, flattening sentence clauses in an endless, undifferentiated stream, and by combining past and present verb tenses within single paragraphs. Finally, his intense focus on objects, describing without naming them, acknowledging their functions, melds representation and speculation.

As Randall Jarrell once noted, in praising the poetry of William Carlos Williams, the too-concrete tends to become abstract. "What is more abstract than a fortuitous collocation of sensations?" he said.

In the twentieth century's second half, existential fiction, whose history I've been tracing here, fell into self-parody. Hemingway's late works are the best-known example. Theorists moved on to structuralism, poststructuralism, deconstruction, and now to the end of theory. Talk about self-consciousness!

Scientists, particularly in the field of artificial intelligence, doubted the very notion of Self apart from physical matter. Most fiction writers returned to an unquestioning dependence on the conventions of realism. But the loose tradition extending from Kierkegaard to Sartre by way of Dostoevsky, Hemingway, Beckett, and others (E. T. A. Hoffman, Kafka, and Poe belong on the list; more recently, Walker Percy, Susan Sontag, Donald Barthelme, Milan Kundera, and J. M. Coetzee), remains compelling. These writers' experiments are instructive to philosophers and novelists, a moving chronicle of an attempt to come to grips with the fundamental natures of world and mind. As the philosopher Maurice Natanson once said, it is a mistake to regard philosophy (and fiction) as a graveyard of dead systems.

Sometimes, after an especially exhausting fight with our mother, my sister would join me on the backyard wall. She'd know I'd have a book in my hands and wasn't likely to say much, so she'd bring her own volume to read. *Flatland* was one of her favorites. She was always good with numbers—one reason Mom's fears never reached her. They didn't add up. "She wants me to be a fairy tale princess, but look at me," she'd say. "I mean, *look at me*—you think she even sees who I am?"

One evening we sat together at dusk, listening to our neighbors' pigeons. We heard the garden hose splashing in the yard next door, water sloshing into shallow plastic bowls, but we couldn't see the boy. The birds' warm, roosting smell, a collective odor like old bedding, wafted our way on the air.

"Are you okay?" I asked Sis.

"I guess. Look at this." She had plucked an old photograph from a family album to use as a bookmark, but then it had caught her eye: our mother, much younger, lying in bed, gripping her rounded belly. "1959," said the date on the back.

"She was pregnant with me," said my sister.

In the picture, my mother appeared to be talking.

"What do you suppose she was trying to tell me?"

I'm reminded of a scene in *Nausea*. The narrator says, "The light grows softer. At this uncertain hour, one felt evening drawing in. Sunday was already past. A pregnant woman leaned against a fair, brutal-looking young man. There, there, look, she said. What? There, the seagulls. He shrugged. There were no seagulls. The sky had become almost pure, a little blush on the horizon. I heard them, listen, they're crying."

The scene is remarkable for its blurring of present and past. Light *grows*, one *felt*—grammatically, *now* has already vanished. It is passing even as we live it. Simultaneously, the future has arrived: a pregnant woman, stuck with an indifferent partner, hears crying, though no seagulls fill the air. No source for the crying exists . . . except for the future, the baby that will soon be born.

Now, I return in memory to see my sister sitting on the wall, bent above the photograph of our mother. Our mother, in the picture, bends to imagine my unborn sister. The setting sunlight grows softer on my face; I hear (or do I just imagine it?) my mother weeping inside the house. Or is it my sister's son I hear—her son who will not be born yet for many years? What possibilities would I offer us all if I could whisper back through time?

"I feel like one of those birds," my sister said, pointing at the coop.

"What do you mean?"

"Trapped. Stupid. Dull."

I'd been reading too much. Overheated by possibilities, I said, "What if the doors popped open? The birds are free."

My sister shook her head.

"Where would they go? North, south, east, west?"

"I don't know."

"What do you think they'll do?"

"I don't know."

"Come on."

"I don't *know*."

"Try."

"Anything?"

"Sure."

"Okay," she said. "One will fly into the desert."

"Yes. Good."

"Another shoots into the clouds."

"All right."

"One just went into the alley and gobbled up a June bug."

For a moment, the scrabbling creatures seem to shed their sadness. And so, for a moment, do we.

# PART THREE

# Literary Craft

# Writing Political Fiction

I'll begin by admitting a flaw in the argument I'm about to make, something I wish our public figures would do more often—and that's the most political statement I'll offer.

I'm going to use two terms interchangeably: the *political* and the *topical*. Of course the political is not always topical and topical matters aren't always open to political debate. But when readers complain of politics ruining literature, they're usually referring to material that quickly dates: a social or cultural issue causing great turmoil in its day, eventually drained of its urgency. When this material starts to go limp, it taints all surrounding ingredients. The whole stew spoils. This is a different concern from writing didactically, which is what we tend to think of when we hear the phrase "political fiction," but I believe it's a more fundamental worry and has much to do with the nature of didacticism.

The fiction writer's challenge, as I see it, is to be a witness to her time without getting trapped in her time. One solution to the problem of topicality is to avoid it, but the deeper puzzle is distinguishing the merely fashionable from current forms of perennial truths. War, for instance. The "war was always there," Ernest Hemingway wrote at the beginning of "In Another Country." War seems destined to blight every era and inscribe itself in each generation's literature. It is both perennial *and* fashionable, but in many literary works it's a dated device, as fleeting and forgettable as the latest dance craze.

The monotony of battle and of political sloganeering can ruin war writing. But the opposite is also true. Despite similarities, wars are unique, each with its specific causes, horrifying events, own vocabulary, technology, and cultural soundtrack. Somehow, the writer must render that uniqueness without making it idiosyncratic; novelty today is tomorrow's cliché. Either way—through over-tending or half-baking—rot sets in.

Scads of books have been written about Vietnam, my generation's signature war, but even now, so soon after that period's passing, only a handful of those books—Tim O' Brien's *The Things They Carried*, as an example—have the whiff of freshness about them. This is not because Tim O'Brien was the best writer in the bunch. Maybe he was, maybe he wasn't, but the case can be made that even among *his* books about Vietnam, only *The Things They Carried* is likely to avoid spoilage.

I'm not going to make that case here. I think it will be easier to appreciate our problem from a greater distance. "Distance" is the key to my argument: distance *from* the topic and distance *in* it—that is, investing the topic with enough momentum to propel it past our time, as NASA swung the Voyager spacecraft around the sun to slingshot it beyond our solar system.

No one expressed the value of distance *from* the topic better than William Wordsworth in his preface to *Lyrical Ballads* in 1802. Famously he said that "poetry is the spontaneous overflow of powerful feeling: it takes its origin from emotion recollected in tranquility." Spontaneous overflow: an immediate response to some issue, personal or political. The immediate, the topical, is essential. It's what gives the writing flavor. But what prevents an emotional tang from dissipating like so much steam is savoring it at length, inhaling it deeply but calmly and with precise deliberation. How this general approach to writing might help us construct a particular work of fiction, we'll consider in a moment.

As for distance *in* the topic, I know of no better formulation of it than Nadine Gordimer's 1980 remark (in an interview with Susan Gardner) that you should "write . . . as if you were already dead." In her specific context, in Johannesburg during Apartheid, Gordimer meant the writer should work boldly without fearing political authorities, censorship, or public reprisals. But the statement transcends its moment and offers us a second bit of general advice: in fiction, we are witnessing our time not for ourselves but for those who will come later, long after the material of our bodies and brains has scattered to places even Voyager can't reach.

Let's turn to two very different writers, Milan Kundera and Virginia Woolf, and watch them practice the principles laid out by Wordsworth and Gordimer. We'll look at how they crafted fictions around the topic of war. With Kundera, we'll consider structural matters. Woolf will guide us through detail and tone.

Milan Kundera centered his 1984 novel *The Unbearable Lightness of Being* around the Soviet invasion of Czechoslovakia in August 1968. The book spends little time discussing specific reasons for the invasion; to some extent, Kundera avoids the risk of spoilage by evading the clutter of the moment whose impact, he knew, would inevitably fade in the media even as it remained historically significant. He places in the novel's foreground a love story; the war remains a backdrop to the intimate joys and pains of Tereza and Tomas. Kundera's tone is philosophical, somewhat abstracted; he composes a meditation on qualities of being, so in a sense his characters are figures in a thought-experiment as opposed to players in a drama.

These three choices—to downplay historical specificity, to emphasize love and sex, and to package the story as a philosophical exercise—are distancing techniques, strategies enabling Kundera to speak of the consequences of war: filtered through abstract categories (lightness and weight), and through romantic play, war's wages can be considered calmly, at a far remove. Yet these choices have risks of their own, the clearest being that it is an obscenity to reduce mass slaughter to the horizon line in a lover's tryst. It is repugnant to reduce people's lives to a game. If Kundera had done nothing more than this, we would not still be reading *The Unbearable Lightness of Being.* The trick is to find the right amount of distance from the topic without losing sight of its integrity. Kundera's mastery of this trick occurs through a particularly modern variation on Wordsworth's dictum: he recollects emotion in tranquility until emotion is forced unexpectedly into the open. The war gets its proper moment in the book—the respect the subject deserves. It explodes. But it does so indirectly when the reader least expects it. Kundera achieves his greatest distance through timing.

The Soviet occupation of Czechoslovakia is essentially the novel's setting. The Russians' presence exacerbates the intimate tensions between Teresa and Tomas by making daily tasks harder than normal and by disrupting friendships, families, careers. In the midst of frequent splits and reunions, Teresa and Tomas buy a dog, a mongrel named Karenin. Karenin is the one constant in their lives, which become increasingly chaotic as the occupation tightens. Kundera does not depict the terrors of oppression; rather, through suggestion and glimpses, a trace of teargas in the air, he uses the occupation as a tension-building device. Following the lover's hardships (many, but not all, caused by the political situation), the reader is barely aware that she has been observing the slow disintegration of a country.

Late in the book, just when Teresa and Tomas seem to have weathered the degradations of the new Czechoslovakia, Karenin takes ill. The reader weeps for the death of a dog. What saves this moment from bathos, and what makes *The Unbearable Lightness of Being* a profoundly political novel, is that our tears for the animal are really tears for a nation. Karenin has witnessed everything the characters have endured. The dog bears on its haunches the history of the occupation, just as a scapegoat embodies a community's sins. This loss, catching us unawares, forcing us to cry just as we were beginning to feel the release of tension, unleashes our rage and grief over war. Until now, the novel's distancing strategies have kept our feelings about the occupation tightly sealed. At the end, the lover's story through the presence of their pet, heretofore taken for granted, becomes the story of the depravity of the twentieth century.

Repression (forced tranquility) and release (powerful emotion): Wordsworth's process is *structurally reversed* here. The material is composed in one direction but ordered in another. Kundera uses repression to get apprehension buzzing and then springs it open indirectly. As a result, readers of *The Unbearable Lightness of Being* will always carry with them the political outrage of Prague in August 1968 even though they may know only dimly what happened there and why.

If Virginia Woolf's prose is deathless, as some readers have claimed, it's because she was dead when she wrote it—dead in Gordimer's sense of consciously writing beyond her time while bundling the breath of her time in every image and sentence. She is the Voyager of Western writers. Listen, as she describes the world's rooms as they exist and will exist without us:

> So with the lamps all put out, the moon sunk, and a thin rain drumming on the roof a downpouring of immense darkness began. Nothing it seemed could survive the flood, the profusion of darkness which, creeping in at keyholes and crevices, stole round window blinds, came into bedrooms, swallowed up here a jug and basin, there a bowl of red and yellow dahlias, there the sharp edges and firm bulk of a chest of drawers. Not only was furniture confounded; there was scarcely anything left of body or mind by which one could say, "This is he" or "This is she."

As with *The Unbearable Lightness of Being*, it is war that dominates the stunning middle section of *To the Lighthouse*, published in 1927, and as in Kundera, it dominates through its absence in the writing. War is scarcely mentioned directly, yet it is never out of mind, even when the only remaining mind seems to be some silent quality of perception in the wind. Woolf writes, "The autumn trees, ravaged as they are, take on the flash of tattered flags kindling in the gloom of cool cathedral caves where gold letters on marble pages describe death in battle and how bones bleach and burn." Here, the specific and datable First World War becomes any war, every war, seen from the endlessly distant perspective of the dead as it leaches into trees, caves, soil. This is war as an element of the earth. This is politics transformed into atmosphere. It is horror beyond the maiming of human limbs, fraying the fabric of space.

Woolf's elegiac tone invests the topical with the timeless. Already, she whispers, every war that will ever be fought has been lost. If this renders the reasons for war meaningless, it does so through a surfeit of meaning. Nothing is without consequence precisely because it *is* ephemeral, not the lone lamp burning in a silent room, not the torn letters in the wastepaper basket, not the stew curdling at room temperature on the stove. If this is so—that *everything* matters, as Woolf's prose insists in tone and minute detail, and in its awareness that everything is passing—then politics and war are no more or less worthy of attention than the footfalls of a cat. Virginia Woolf found a place for politics in fiction. Its place was nowhere and everywhere. Just like the dead.

> Night after night, summer and winter, the torment of storms, the arrow-like stillness of fine weather, held their court without interference. Listening (had there been any one to listen) from the upper rooms of the empty house only gigantic chaos streaked with lightning could have been heard tumbling and tossing.

Do you hear the war? Its terrifying clatter? Its even more distressing stillness? After the fighting ceases, and Lily Briscoe returns to this empty house, she asks herself, "What does it mean then, what can it all mean?" She is thinking of the war, of the bad politics of the modern age. But she is also thinking of lost intimacies, missed opportunities, the currents of time. Politics simply takes its place among other needling concerns.

The didactic impulse, to which we are all prone, seeks an answer to Lily's question, and the writer who surrenders to the temptation to provide a direct answer is the writer we have in mind when we complain that politics ruins fiction. The response to Lily's question, Lily decides, is "Nothing, nothing—nothing that she could express at all."

We should not misread Virginia Woolf here, think her a nihilist or mistake her for an apolitical writer. Nothing determines the kind of Something we get. That "Nothing" may very well be the answer to "What can it all mean?" makes the writing of fiction, which is our flawed way of both asking and trying to satisfy our need to ask the question—one of the most doggedly human, and political, acts of which we are capable.

# American Speech, American Silence

Chappaquiddick

The word bears strong associations for people my age and older (I was born in 1955). Like *Watergate* and *Three Mile Island*, *Chappaquiddick* has assumed a life beyond its circumstances. Succeeding generations of Americans may not know precisely what happened on the night of July 18, 1969, in a tidal channel off the coast of Massachusetts—still, they grasp the word's lingering cultural significance.

At approximately 11:15 that night, Senator Edward ("Ted") Kennedy left a party on Chappaquiddick Island in the company of a young woman named Mary Jo Kopechne (Kennedy's wife had not gone to the party; he claimed she was ill). He was driving his mother's Oldsmobile, the keys to which he'd obtained from his chauffer. Later, at an inquest into the death of Mary Jo Kopechne, Kennedy testified that his chauffer was "enjoying the fellowship" of others at the party at the time Kennedy wished to leave, so he did not trouble the poor fellow to take him home. Ms. Kopechne "was desirous of leaving, if I would be kind enough to drop her back at her hotel," Kennedy said. Later, investigators learned that Kopechne had left her hotel key at the party, along with her purse, and had told none of her friends she was leaving with the senator.

Kennedy testified that he made a wrong turn at Dike Road (a simple mistake—he was not intoxicated, he said) and, in the dark, drove into the Poucha Pond, landing the car upside down underwater. He was able to swim free. Ms. Kopechne was not. He claimed he called her name repeatedly, tried three or four times to dive to where she was trapped, rested on the bank for a quarter of an hour, and then returned on foot to the party. He said he saw no houses on the way. Otherwise, he would have phoned the police. In fact, four houses lined the route he took, one of which, just 150 yards from the scene of the accident, had its porch lights on, according to its resident, Sylvia Malm.

Back at the party, Kennedy did not pick up the telephone. Instead, he drew aside a group of close friends and associates, cautioned them not to tell anyone what had happened, and took them to the spot where the car had left the road. The men dove into the water but failed to find Ms. Kopechne. They told Kennedy he must report the incident; he led them to believe he would.

Afterward, he went to his hotel (claiming, in one account, that he swam there, five hundred feet across the channel; in another account, he said he'd caught a lift from someone). He fell into bed. "I almost tossed and turned," he testified. "Almost" is an odd word choice here. "I had not given up hope that, by some miracle, Mary Jo would have escaped from the car."

At the inquest, the hotel owner said he got a call from Kennedy at 2:55 a.m. complaining he had just been awakened by a party in another room. Witnesses said they saw Kennedy the following morning at 7:30, chatting casually with people and showing no signs of distress. It was only after the senator's associates met him at 8:00, learned that he had not reported the accident, and initiated a heated conversation with him that Kennedy reached for a phone. He did not call the police right away. He contacted friends and lawyers, seeking advice on what to do.

Meanwhile, a pair of fishermen had discovered the sunken car and alerted authorities. A professional diver, John Farrar, found Mary Jo Kopechne's body in the Oldsmobile at 8:45. Farrar testified, "She didn't drown. She died of suffocation in her own air void. It took her at least three or four hours to die. I could have had her out of that car in twenty-five minutes after I got the call. But he didn't call."

Kennedy pleaded guilty to leaving the scene of an accident and received a two-month suspended sentence based on his character and previous reputation, despite the findings of the Massachusetts Supreme Judicial Court that he had "failed to exercise due care" while operating the vehicle, that he was "at least negligent and possibly reckless" for "some reason not apparent from his testimony," his testimony being that he was not drunk, and that his negligence "appears to have contributed to the death of Mary Jo Kopechne."

The Kopechne family brought no charges against the senator, receiving as a settlement more than ninety thousand dollars from him as well as fifty thousand from his insurance company. "We figured that people would think we were looking for blood money," said the Kopechnes. Eventually, they vanished from public view. Kennedy went on to a storied political career, serving nearly fifty years in Washington, D.C., lauded as a lion of the United States Senate when he died in 2009, praised, among other things, for championing women's rights.

Chappaquiddick is not mentioned in Joyce Carol Oates's 1992 novel *Black Water*, but the word rings like a funeral bell in the minds of readers old enough to remember the incident. The novel depicts a human tragedy based on the life and death of Mary Jo Kopechne, yet the book's unspoken word chimes its deepest theme: American language. Oates asks, Who has a voice in American culture and who doesn't? Among the many tensions in the story raised by the brief encounter between "Kelly Kelleher" and "The Senator"—youth and age, innocence and experience, private and public, female and male—it is silence and speech that most obsesses Oates. Language can shape or bury our identities.

Though Kelly's voice *does* bubble up through the novel—the book exists to *give* her a voice—she is essentially a silent creature in a word-littered landscape. As pictured in *Black Water*, American culture is a pool of "decay," literally and conceptually, smelling of sewage; it is glutted with language used to manipulate, bully, persuade, and cajole. A person can drown in it.

When asked by her best friend why she is leaving the party with the senator, Kelly, caught in a socially awkward moment, is "unable to say." She is the kind of young woman who always carries condoms in her purse, hoping for an opportunity to use one, but when an opportunity arises, "there [are] no words." She is eager, even prepared, but too shy to assert herself (all her life, magazine ads have assured her she is flawed if her skin is not perfect, and her father once told her she had a "defect" because her eyes needed correction). When she *does* speak—"I think we're lost, Senator"—no one listens. At the moment the Toyota careens into the water, she is unable to call to the man behind the wheel: she doesn't know him well enough to be on a first-name basis with him, but to keep calling him "Senator" is inappropriately formal at this point (when she's got his beery-kiss taste in her mouth).

Her companion, a public man and a political leader, is *all* words—"forever campaigning," Oates writes. He always speaks with "the air of one delivering self-evident truths." He is "in the habit of making queries that [are] in fact statements." He will not let his judgment be crossed, though he is often wrong (he misidentifies a Beatles song on the car radio; he shouts, "Here's our turn," missing it while wildly sloshing his vodka on Kelly's thigh). When the car flips in the water, he repeats, "Oh God Oh God," not in misery or as prayer, but as a kind of aggressive sales pitch to the Almighty.

*Black Water* depicts the meeting of words and wordlessness, of power and helplessness. Before getting into the car with Kelly, the senator kisses her at the party. This shuts her up: "The giddy smell of alcohol pungent between them . . . that tongue thick enough to choke you." Kelly has *already* drowned, long before she plunges into the night's black pond.

Young Woman as Vessel, filled to bursting with the culture's cant: this image anchors the novel's circular structure, which eddies like a whirlpool around the accident and Kelly's death.

And what is the nature of the language flooding this eager, silent girl? To begin with, the language of politics. In college, Kelly's honors thesis was entitled "Jeffersonian Idealism and 'New Deal' Pragmatism: Liberal Strategies in Crisis." Presumably, the senator—the subject of Kelly's thesis—has built his career on phrases such as these. Naively, Kelly believes his words define moral principles and interests. For the senator, political language is less about morals than expediency. "It's a lonely life, hearing your own voice in your ears so much," he tells Kelly at the party, using his world-weary status—*poor me, it's such a burden to be the spokesperson for my generation*—as a slyly seductive ploy.

There is the language of advertising: "Acne can occur at any time not just adolescence!" Self-conscious about her flaws, susceptible to manufacturers who say they'll fix her, Kelly ties her physical identity to the needs of the marketplace.

There is the language of those who claim to divine all answers. They seek our trust in order to sell magazines, newspapers, books: "Scorpio . . . For once demand YOUR wishes and get YOUR own way!" These hucksters foster the illusion of knowing us personally while assuring us we're just like all the others. We *belong.*

There is the language of romance, of radio love songs: "She was the girl, she was the one."

There is the language of soft-core pornography, titillating us into thinking we must be missing the world's continuous orgy: "The flawlessly beautiful woman . . . lies languorously sprawled as in a bed . . . breasts, belly, pubic area subtly defined by shimmering folds in the cloth. . . . [She] gazes up at him not required to smile in invitation, for she herself *is* the invitation."

There is the language of nationalism—catch phrases triggering automatic responses: *beacon of freedom, honor,* and *glory.* The Fourth of July.

Chappaquiddick.

Why does it matter if we do or do not pay strict attention to language? Oates begins and ends with Ted Kennedy's obfuscating testimony: the words we hear each day, particularly from our leaders, are mostly lies, or they are used to promote or protect untruths.

In the car, leaving the party with the senator, Kelly thinks that the two of them "had been talking companionably together, and they had been laughing easily together, like old friends, like the most casual of old friends." In her head she composes this story while trying discreetly "to steady The Senator's hand so that the remains of his vodka-and-tonic [won't] splash over the rim of the plastic cup he held as he drove." Kelly, raised on the romance of "she's the one," of being chosen by the Great Man, *wants* to believe in love at first sight. The culture *tells* her to believe in it (the Gross National Product *depends* on her gullibility).

A simple word, "like." Innocent-sounding. *Like* old friends. But the word blinds Kelly to the fact that she is caught in an out-of-control

Toyota with a married, drunk old man, whose act of *choosing* her, under these circumstances, damns his judgment.

Later, having abandoned Kelly in the car (escaping by using her body as leverage), the senator fears he would "never [be] elected president of the United States after all . . . the terror of it washing over him, sick, sick in his guts, swaying like a drunk running across the highway." Here, the word *like* sheds its innocence. It forms the core of the false story the senator will tell himself and others—he's not a drunk, he insists, really he's not, he's simply *like* a drunk. Subsequently, he will embellish the story, concocting a fiction for his legal protection. Reality is what we say it is, as long as those who disagree with us have been silenced.

With carefully placed abstractions ("The Senator" could be *any* powerful man, in any era), Oates urges us not to read this story as the tale of two people only, but to see it as a parable for our time, a tragedy that will recur—in part, because of the misconceptions, manipulations, and principles of inequity built into American language.

The tragedies are not just personal. The senator smashes his Toyota into a guardrail. The guardrail, "rusted to lacework, appeared to give way without retarding the car's speed at all." So, in fact, the rail is improperly named. It doesn't do what it says it will do. It guards nothing, except perhaps—in the most perfunctory manner—the county's legal obligations. The road, no longer maintained, "should have been officially shut down: ROAD OUT." But there is no such sign. No language exists where words of warning *should* be present. This is a massive public failing, a failure of political leadership. Rather than fix the problem, local officials will rush to conceal it, after the fact, with handy phrases.

None of which is news to us. At the end of the nineteenth century, Joseph Conrad's *Heart of Darkness* illustrated the coruscating effects on language of the marriage of nationalism and trade. (We "should be like a beacon on the road towards better things, a center for trade, of course, but also for humanizing, improving, instructing [others]," says a Company man, his self-promoting idealism the perfect cover and justification for Kurtz's outburst: "Exterminate the brutes!") In his 1946 essay "Politics and the English Language," George Orwell warned us how badly Western civilization had slipped.

What Oates's novel reveals is how fully *denial* and *deniability* have infested American speech. And how inured we are to it. The fact that we are no longer outraged by public lies, that our leaders use them constantly with a nod and a wink, is the most damning possible indictment of contemporary American culture.

In *Black Water* we meet a conservative politician who calls himself "pro-choice"—"the key to America's future salvation was abortion [he said], abortion in the right demographic quarters, blacks, Hispanics, welfare mothers." If the term "pro-choice" can be used this way, to mask racism or genocide, if America's public speech becomes nothing more than code, aimed at divided constituencies who know exactly what they are hearing, but under the clever cover of deniability, then democracy has imploded.

As the story of an innocent young woman seduced by power, Oates's novel treads familiar water. As a thinly disguised retelling of the Chappaquiddick incident, it risks the titillation of a roman a clef. But as a parable of speech and silence, *Black Water* achieves the freshness of myth, perennially relevant.

When Ted Kennedy died in September 2009, Oates examined his life in an article in Britain's *Guardian* newspaper. "It might be argued that Senator Kennedy's career as one of the most influential of 20th century Democratic politicians . . . was a consequence of his notorious behavior at Chappaquiddick bridge in July 1969," she wrote. The "Renaissance concept of the 'fortunate fall' may be relevant here: one 'falls' as Adam and Eve fell; one sins and is forgiven, provided that one remakes one's life." Ironically, "appealing to his lawyer and not rather seeking emergency help for the trapped Mary Jo Kopechne would seem, in retrospect, to have been a felicitous move. If Kennedy had summoned aid, he would very likely have given police officers self-incriminating evidence, which might have involved charges of vehicular manslaughter or homicide." The remarkable career that followed would never have occurred.

The "fortunate fall" is an archetype replayed in every culture in every historical period. Inevitably, for the fallen individual to be redeemed, Oates says, "innocent individuals figure . . . as ritual sacrifices" in the drama. Like the scapegoat bearing the community's sins, slated to die, certain individuals are chosen from time to time to be exiled or killed for the sake of a greater good ("she's the one," she "*is* the invitation"). Naturally, the chosen one never has a voice, can never refute the waves of language baptizing her and shaping her role.

In the *Guardian* piece, Oates asks, "If one weighs the life of a single young woman against the accomplishments of the man President Obama has called the greatest Democratic senator in history, what is one to think?"

*Black Water* forces this question on us. Further, the novel challenges us to wonder *who* and *what* gets sacrificed, generation after generation, and for what purposes. How do we prepare these ritual offerings? We fashion a Kelly Kelleher in our image, telling her what to believe, what to buy, whom to vote for, constructing a vocabulary for her. She believes it is *her* language, when in fact it's a gag meant to silence her: "that tongue thick enough to choke you."

Once we have made her, we court her and then we cast her off. What is it we are losing when we abandon her and leave her trapped? When her lungs fill with black water in a "shallow ditch" engorged with America's detritus: "a broken dinette table, the front wheel of an English racing bicycle, the headless naked body of a flesh-pink doll . . . [with a] hole between the shoulders like a bizarre mutilated vagina where the head had been wrenched off"? What part of ourselves are we killing? And for what? For whom?

Only by parsing the languages of power and words habitually silenced can we answer these questions. Our reluctance to face the answers is exemplified, in Oates's necessary novel, as a road rarely traveled, with a fetid sewage dump waiting at the end.

*Not now. Not like this,* Kelly thinks once the senator has left her to die.

But yes, America. Now. Like this. Start talking.

# The Black Butterfly

"Making love with your socks on. That's fatal. It can never work," Gabriel García Márquez insisted when an interviewer asked him once if he had any superstitions. "I believe that superstitions, or what are commonly called such, correspond to natural forces which rational thinking, like that of the West, has rejected," he added.

More than their North American counterparts, writers from Central and South America have studied superstition, free will, and fate, noted their correspondences and countervailing currents, and made provocative narrative art from their intersections. For García Márquez and his compatriots, these speculations are not trifling nor are they literary games. They reveal the human situation, complicating our views of time and the meaning of mortal affairs.

Bad luck, those socks. Why? *They can never work.* García Márquez makes it clear that, more than just ill omens, the socks are practical or aesthetic mistakes: *By God, you want to leap into my bed, you'll kick those damn things off!*

If superstitions "correspond to natural forces," we should be able to find rational causes for them. If they are, in fact, grounded in "reality," would that make them any less mysterious or profound? Much of the power of Latin American narratives springs from this question.

"Because Cortés lands on a day specified in the ancient writings; because he is dressed in black, because his armor is silver in color, a certain *ugliness* of the strangers taken as a group—for these reasons Montezuma considers Cortés to be Quetzalcoatl, the great god who left Mexico many years before on a raft of snakes, vowing to return," says

Donald Barthelme in his magical retelling of the historical and mythical forces forming modern Mexico. (Barthelme was a Texan much influenced by his neighbors to the south.) His paragraph demonstrates how superstition and coincidence are often mistakenly interpreted as inevitability.

An illusion of inevitability shapes *identity*; this illusion is the lynchpin of narrative art. A complex understanding of the relationships between history and myth amid the clatter of cultural smash-ups is the birthright of most Latin American writers. *Identity* is their primary subject, to which fate, free will, and superstition are simultaneously central and subordinate.

Identities form in faulty environments. A muddy mix.

In *Chronicle of a Death Foretold*, one of his many meditations on narrative, García Márquez exposes the porous ground on which stories-of-origin stand. Of a particularly important day in the history of an insular community, the novel's narrator says, "Many people coincided in recalling that it was a radiant morning with a sea breeze.... But most agreed that the weather was funereal ... a thin drizzle was falling." Later, he offers a concrete explanation for why the townspeople's memories clashed: the whistle of a paddle-wheeler chuffing upriver "let off a shower of compressed steam as it passed by the docks, and it soaked those who were closest to the edge." No wonder some folks recalled a light drizzle. Natural forces can blur into superstitious thinking, especially in retrospect—*It was a terribly fateful day, so it* had *to be funereal and wet.*

In the blur of memory and myth, questions occur. To what degree are we bound by natural forces? To what extent do we mold them to suit our needs? In formulating our answers, is *mis*-understanding as crucial as grasping the facts? Is a superstitious belief, if it has the power to move someone, a force unfolding exactly as it must?

In 1880 the peripatetic and astonishing Brazilian novelist Machado de Assis—one of García Márquez's early influences—published a book later translated into English as *Epitaph of a Small Winner* or *The Posthumous Memoirs of Bras Cubas*. With its fragmented form and acid irony, it seemed to declare itself a fresh narrative example for a New

World. In this collision of cultures and beliefs (between Europe and America), what *are* we if not fragmented, it asked; how should we see our intermarried selves, *them* and *not-them*, if not through a scrim of irony?

Bras Cubas speaks from the grave. He has decided to start the book with his death rather than his birth, he says, because the story will then gain in "merriment." Apparently, his ectoplasmic state has freed him from the stuffy conventions of European literature. What are the implications of this for "character" and "identity"?

Cubas tells us he was educated in Lisbon. Then he returned to Brazil. His identity is a volatile mix of native New World pride and European snobbery. The combination saddles him with massive self-hatred: common enough, in the history of the Americas.

In one early scene in the book, a black butterfly drifts through an open window, startling two Brazilian women who are sitting with Cubas. Bound by native superstitions, they interpret the butterfly as a dark omen. "Superior" in knowledge and manner because of his worldly education, Cubas laughs at their beliefs (which, at one time, he would have shared). Later, the pesky creature lands on a painted portrait of his father, a man also drawn to Europe but who nevertheless retained his cultural roots. From the canvas, the butterfly flutters its wings at Cubas in a "mocking way" (as Cubas mocks his father's attachment to traditional customs). Angered, Cubas smashes the insect. Immediately, he's seized with regret.

He tries to help the wounded butterfly. It seems he is not entirely free of his past, or of superstitions, after all—especially in the glare of his father's frank and unforgiving gaze.

Eventually, from standing too near an open window he contracts pneumonia (perhaps the butterfly *was* a bad omen, after all). Publicly, he blames fate for his illness—it's a case of poor luck. Later, he grudgingly acknowledges to the reader that he may have had some agency in the matter. He says he didn't take care of himself. (On a larger scale, *all of Brazil* is the cause of his disease: frequently, throughout the country, pneumonia spread rapidly among the uncared-for slave populations, and then to wider communities. There is fate, and there is fate, the inevitable, if unintended, consequences of power and greed.)

Cubas begins a romance with a woman named Virgilia. "It was our fate to fall in love," he insists. But then, like García Márquez discussing his socks, Cubas qualifies our understanding of cosmic forces. "Now that all the social laws forbade it . . . we truly loved each other."

The fact is, his passion for Virgilia rises only *after* she has married another man. Competitive, jealous of others, he desires her as "mine."

His grasping reveals a sad instability, a deeply shaky self, as does his narrative boasting. A defiant rejection of European literature? An assertion of New World identity? Listen harder. "I do not wish to add fuel to the fire of criticism," he admits, not at all free of public opinion (American *or* European), the status quo with its deeply held prejudices and simplistic beliefs. Despite efforts to convince himself that he fully controls his life, Cubas keeps glancing behind him, dreading the black butterfly.

Much of what happens in our lives is socially and culturally determined, whether or not we recognize the causes. This is the lesson of *Chronicle of a Death Foretold*. The story centers on the murder of one Santiago Nasar, a killing announced well in advance among members of a small community by gossip, innuendo, social cues, and apparent portents and signs. These last are either passed off as coincidence or interpreted as an alignment of the stars. Everyone in the village is free to stop the killing. Or are they?

On the morning of his death, Nasar already had the "face" of a dead man, someone says later. Another person confirms "he already looked like a ghost." A woman who accidentally brushed his hand that morning says it was "cold and stony, like that of a dead man." How do you aid a walking corpse?

Dreams, prophecies, superstitions weave the town's social fabric. Additionally, a story told with hindsight naturally acquires the illusion of inevitability. Details overlooked at the time accrue enormous importance later.

Narrative *is* Fate—a story can't violate its own terms; it doesn't exist apart from them.

Each chapter in the novel, exploring Nasar's demise, employs the diction of a particular profession or realm of knowledge: journalism, history, law, medicine, and gossip. This structure reveals the self-fulfilling nature of any limited perspective. From a legal point of view, Nasar was killed "in a legitimate defense of honor" (after all, this is the culture of machismo). In that sense, he *had* to die. Afterward, the autopsy, itself an act of butchery ("It was as if we killed him all over again after he was dead") revealed that, following a case of poorly healed hepatitis, "he had only a few years of life left to live." Nasar was fated to die young, anyway. What this means (if anything), and whether it matters, depends on how you view it. And how you view it is determined by your culture, your social background within it.

Ultimately, the woman who "caused" Nasar's murder (he was killed in defense of her honor) renounces society and persists in a self-made limbo, a kind of death-in-life. Fate personified, the end in the beginning, the butterfly in the caterpillar, woven to the bottom of a leaf, disguising its identity from those that would feed on it or, heeding superstitions, destroy it.

Some facts about butterflies: their sole purpose is to reproduce (unlike bees, they are poor pollinators); of one hundred laid eggs, generally only about 2 percent survive; their wings are fragile—the appearance of graceful freedom, then, is a grand illusion; their eyes consist of thousands of hexagonal shaped omatidea, allowing them to see in virtually every direction at once; however, because their brains are so small, unable to unscramble the complexities of their visual apparatus, what they actually register is a blur—light, color, motion; black butterflies, common in the southern Americas, winter as pupas, using parsley, dill, fennel, and Queen Anne's lace as host plants; they emerge in the spring, a time of new portents; they use their markings to mimic *Battus philenor* (the pipevine swallowtail), bad-tasting to predatory birds; frequently, they can be found in tropical libraries, pressed, along with wildflowers, between the pages of dusty old tomes.

In the New World's Judeo-Christian tradition, an inheritance from Europe (our fate?), pilgrims ask to be inscribed in the Book of Life. This suggests belief in an unfolding pattern, as complex as that on a butterfly's wing, a story with openings for fresh characters and events, but whose trajectory (presumably salvation) is fixed. Otherwise, why would we want to be inserted into the narrative?

How flexible *is* the plot of our lives? Can a story line ever be tweaked? If so, what does that do to the ending? Persistently, Latin American writers, blessed or cursed with unusually intricate cultural histories, have approached these questions with insight, patience, and wit.

Generally, they report that the Book of Life contains flaky edges, missing pages, and a rather loose spine. It might as well be bound by restless snakes. And what of the blurry-eyed creatures pressed into the center of its story, fretting about forces beyond their control, while glancing in all directions—not really seeing—and frantic to reproduce?

As Bras Cubas grumbles, perhaps "the main defect of this book is you, reader."

# The Babies in the Room

On Christmas Eve 2012, as one of my stocking-stuffers, my mother gave me a desk calendar featuring articles from the satirical newspaper *The Onion*: fake horoscopes, parodies of world leaders and celebrities, twisted commentary on cultural trends and pathologies. Every day during the first four months of 2013, I dutifully tore the pages off the calendar, keeping track of the dates, laughing at the jokes. A few weeks ago, for the first time in many months, I happened to notice the calendar on a kitchen shelf. It had stopped, which meant *I* had stopped, on Wednesday, May 8. *The Onion*'s May 8 headline read, "Journey of Self-Discovery Leads Man to Realization He Doesn't Care."

The accompanying article began, "Three months after setting off down a long spiritual path to find himself, 38-year-old Corey Larson arrived at the conclusion Tuesday that he does not care. Larson said of his soul-searching journey, 'Fuck it. Fuck it all.' [He] briefly considered writing a self-help book to make the journey easier for others, but decided that he also didn't give two shits about whether other people arrived at the same conclusion he did."

Before going any further, we should note the warning to writers here who think the world is eagerly waiting for their stories of self-discovery when in fact most of the world couldn't give two shits. I'll keep that warning in mind as I proceed. Also worth noting: the brilliant concept of the *Onion* piece isn't really what makes its humor click. It's a simple detail: the man's spiritual non-awakening occurred on a "Tuesday."

Simple details tell us the story. Or part of it, anyway. I lost track of 2013 on a Wednesday. Five weeks later, on a Sunday afternoon, when my

*Onion* horoscope read, "You're starting to think that maybe the funny nose and glasses won't actually be enough to hide you when Jesus returns in all his glory," my mother died. That I abandoned the calendar, her gift, five weeks earlier tells me this, in hindsight: May 8 was the day I accepted after months of denial that my mother *was* going to die, and my depression was such that Time, the future, anticipating anything at all, mattered not a whit. "Fuck it, fuck it all," I thought and still sometimes think.

But that word, "sometimes," is important here. It's like a coordinating conjunction, a continuation, in the middle of a sentence. The stopping of Time altogether suggests the end of narrative. Yet we are Time's creatures, *in* and *of* its muddy flood; we tell stories in Time, and as long as its movement *hasn't* stopped for us, not today, we make narrative links. For nearly all of us, narratives begin in the family womb. My mother's gift of the calendar and its sudden halt for the two of us on particular dates helped me experience, viscerally, what had been previously only an abstraction: the knowledge that Time—its pressure and management—is one of the essential aspects of structuring stories.

Within a month of my mother's death, I helped my eighty-six-year-old father put the house he had shared with her on the market (he'd moved into an assisted living facility), and pack up sixty-four years' worth of accumulated objects for an estate sale. While scouring closets and cupboards, I discovered my mother's 2013 calendar, Scotch-taped inside a kitchen cabinet containing all her prescription pills, emergency telephone numbers, and old Kleenex tissues still smelling of her, imprinted with her lipstick. The first three months of the calendar were marked, in her precise handwriting, with cramped notices of social engagements, upcoming doctor appointments, and reminders of the housekeepers' schedule. Her time was full. It began to run out in mid-March, by which date, in fact, she'd be starting to fail. A blank spot on June 16, the day she'd die. The calendar noted that on June 21, the day we buried her, "Summer begins."

To the writer in me, nearly dormant with grief, my mother's plans, followed by mocking blank squares, exposed Time's limitations: while essential, Time is not ample enough for *story*. And I confess: I was looking for a story that day, a continuation. Something other than "Fuck it."

Staring at the calendar, at the labels on the half-empty bottles of pills (*Two per day for thirty-three days, refill expires in August—the pressure of Time*), I realized that Time is merely a story's through-line—a guide perhaps to nowhere, certainly not to the beating heart of the matter.

So. What else do we need for story besides the needle-and-thread of chronology? Besides simple details, like tissues smeared with lipstick?

Here's a brief excerpt of a journal I kept while helping my father pack up his house. It's raw and unedited, the kind of stuff the world doesn't give two shits about, nor should it. I hadn't looked at it again until I began to consider this essay: "We sat in my sister's old bedroom, my father on the bed, me on a stack of boxes. When he was ready, I pulled other taped boxes from a closet, the word 'Office' scrawled across them in black Marks-A-Lot. My mother's handwriting. I pulled off the tape and opened the flaps. One by one, with my foot, I pushed the boxes gently toward my father so he could see what was inside. He bent, groaning a little. 'This has no earthly value,' he said, holding up, one after another, the thin mementoes of his life: a plaque honoring five years of service with the Sinclair Oil and Gas Company, a ten-year pin, twenty, a photograph of his retirement party, my mother, smiling, toasting him with a flute of champagne. 'No value at all,' he said. 'Just take it all away.' 'You're sure?' I asked. He replied, 'No earthly reason to keep it.' No. My mother had been the one to save and document, to chronicle our lives. She had been our witness. Our storyteller.

"The plaques and pictures I hauled to the Dumpster in the alley until I stuffed the bin and had to stumble to other Dumpsters several yards away—over a dozen trips, tears in my eyes, my mother's name on my lips, not in gratitude for cherishing our lives' humble transitions, but in shame at my undoing of her efforts."

I'm not moved now to analyze the journal in any fashion except to say that whatever fragile structure it has—written on the fly—is grammatical. The grammar of correct usage, nouns and verbs and syntax, certainly. But more than that, I think: my *family*'s grammar, the way we talk to one another, the way we sit together, our bodies' dialogue—my foot pushing the boxes at my father "gently," as if I had no agency in the matter, as if the box were moving on its own, *I had nothing to do with this, Dad, please don't make me do this*, what we understand without speaking and what we fail to understand, my father's drone, "No earthly value." It's not just the nuts-and-thorns of this phrase that are so familiar to me, so ingrained in the stories I write. It's the grammar of my father's being-in-the-world, his movements, the speed of his metabolism, all of which I share, along with those of my mother, in my DNA. It's his melancholy squint at life—certainly part of my family's deep structure. I know that. I know it better when I write.

When we think about story structure, we tend to think about incidents and the interplay of memory and imagination; we fret about *meaning*, trying to ascribe it to what has happened to us. What I'm arguing is that we need to trust the movements of our sentences, mimicking the movements of our bodies and minds, which carry within them our families' cadences, the syntax of its talk, its comic or tragic tones, the qualified dodges, like little parenthetical dances, of negotiating family spaces, rooms, landscapes, houses.

When we structure a story it's experience, not meaning, we try to impart. Let me amend that: experience *as much as* meaning. Meaning's abstract, easily dispersed (like our grasp of Time's movement); experience (what we fill our time *with*, and *how* we do it) is physical as well as spiritual/emotional/endorphin-fueled, painful, and for that reason, remains. It remains in the body even when the mind begins to lose it.

Experience, including linguistic use, is rooted in the beating of the heart, in syncopation, nerve firings, reaction times: a system of grammar fed to us by family through genetics, unconscious habits, formal rituals, speech . . . already, we have all the structure we need. We find it by writing it, experiencing it in the concerted motion of brain and hand, mind and body, our personal music.

Here's what my journal showed me: even our rough drafts have shapes, edges, duration—and *that's* where to look, long before you think your scribbles have stumbled into meaning.

Self-discovery? Who gives a shit? Really.

Writing is not a matter of using words as tools to uncover some buried truth. Writing is self-*creation*. And, in fact, our words aren't tools at all. They're inheritances from history, culture, family. We inherit traits and dispositions, pacing and stamina, tics and trigger-reactions, all reflected in the rhythms of our speaking and writing, and out of them we fashion a persona, a way of being and acting in the world. We fashion, revising often, a history for ourselves. The structures of the stories we make (stories we *live* on the page, moving, pausing, stuttering, screaming) are embedded in this process until the days of the calendar run out. Which they will, sooner than you think.

Simple details, moving in Time, fixed by family grammar.

*There was no earthly value to the lipsticked tissue with which I marked the day this sorrowful summer began.*

On the day she died, my mother moved in and out of lucidity. She thought she'd come to the hospital to give birth, first to me, then to my sister. These were the experiences pressed in the folds of her body like seals into wax, even as her mind was letting go of the self. "Are the babies in the room?" she asked.

A little later, she said, "I'm trying to figure it out."

And then: "This wasn't supposed to happen to me."

*Are the babies in the room? I'm trying to figure it out. This wasn't supposed to happen to me.*

These three sentences are all anyone needs to tell a family story.

# PART FOUR

# Freeing the Imagination through Craft

# Mother

Motherhood is Grace Paley's great subject. It was her gift to invest maternity with the urgency of mass movements for justice. In Paley's stories and poems, motherhood is a public and political obligation, as well as domestic labor.

It is also our strongest reminder of mortality. Birth is the beginning of death. This simple shorthand provided Paley a principle of compression that gave her short pieces the heft of novels and the scope of epic drama. "Just this morning I looked out the window . . . and saw that the little sycamores the city had dreamily planted a couple of years before the kids were born had come that day to the prime of their lives," says one of Paley's mothers, in a story called "Wants." A generation has matured in the space of this sentence, signaled by the growth of the trees, seeds to saplings to shade. A woman's life has all but passed. We sense the empty nest behind her, implied by her solitary act of looking out the window. Equating the city's undertaking—"dreamily" planting trees—with children's births ties communal attempts at improvement with nurturing of the most intimate nature.

The sycamores, now in the "prime of their lives," remain "little" in the woman's mind. An awareness of change (while lost in memory) carries us back to origins. It seems that "just this morning" the trees have "come" to their prime. Insistence on the present—*me, here, now!*—stresses how fleeting the present will be.

"I want . . . to be a different person," the woman thinks, later in the story. Her wish will be granted the moment she makes it. Time will ensure its fulfillment. In Paley's fierce syntactic hug, time is a verb tugging all nouns and dependent clauses toward the end of the tale. Thus, the urgency in intimacy, the drive to fix the world while we can.

If compression were just a rhetorical tactic in Paley's work, the link between motherhood and activism would be no more deeply inscribed than a slogan on a sign at a rally: "Babies Not Bombs!"

Compression can be a device for reducing ideas to aphorisms. It can also be—as in Paley's writing—literary bone marrow, an instinctive understanding of life, realized in a particular style.

Paley's poem "On Occasion," a meditation on aging, begins:

> I forget the names of my friends
> and the names of the flowers in
> my garden    my friends remind me
> Grace    it's us    the flowers just
> stand there stunned by the mid-
> summer day

The poem's first act of compression is to equate flowers with friends (using a simple "and"). Grace's colloquial voice fuses with the lyrical voice of pastoral poetry: flowers are an age-old symbol of the fragility of beauty and life. The garden consists not only of the flowers Grace has planted but of the friends she has gathered over many, many years. Now, midlife has tipped into old age. Note the shock of the line break, "mid- /summer." The last half of that word is sliding into autumn. Too soon, too soon!

Grace remembers:

> A long time ago my mother said
> darling    there are also wild flowers
> but look    these I planted

In distinguishing "wild flowers" from those she "planted," the mother taught her daughter the importance of cultivating friends, creating community, in what would otherwise be a wilderness.

But now Grace is starting to forget.

Having lost the flowers' names, she stands and contemplates their "fat round faces," like the faces of babies. All at once, the yard is teeming with infants. The poem's connections—*flowers–friends–community*—extend now to *children. Generations.*

The last stanza reverses the terms of the first. "I forget," the poem began—a lost thought. But now, "suddenly before thought," before the *possibility* of forgetting, Grace hears the word "ZINNIA." It comes floating, unbidden, into her mind, preconscious, rooted more deeply in her skull than memory's labored processes.

> . . . along came a sunny
> summer breeze    they [the flowers] swayed and
> lightly bowed    so I said    Mother

One last act of compression: *zinnia* equals *mother.* The poem's flower imagery, ending in *mother*, connects the natural world, friends, community, children, language, even preconsciousness. Everything swaying and bowing (respect, fragility, the pliant bones of creeping old age).

"Mother" is the poem's final word. Everything comes to rest in her, where everything began—in the white space ("before thought") prior to the poem's first line. Birth is the beginning of death.

A sketch appears in Paley's 1985 short story collection, *Later the Same Day*, entitled simply "Mother." It begins:

> One day I was listening to the AM radio. I heard a song: "Oh, I Long to See My Mother in the Doorway." By God! I said, I understand that song. I have often longed to see my mother in the doorway. As a matter of fact, she did stand frequently in various doorways looking at me.

Once again, a specific moment serves to layer years. The phrase "various doorways" is the key to Paley's compression here, allowing her to display her mother at several periods in her life. Doorways are passages, a potent image of change, of movement and time, therefore of longing.

Paley recalls her youth, her dawning of political consciousness. She says her activities worried her mother:

At the door of the kitchen she said, You never finish your lunch. You run around senselessly. What will become of you?

Then she died.

Naturally for the rest of my life I longed to see her, not just in doorways, in a great number of places.

*Compression* is hardly the word for this leap forward in time, the breathtaking and unprepared-for suddenness of "Then she died." The startling effect is created by the *juxtaposition* of an extended anecdote followed by a flat, emotionally precise statement.

"What will become of you?"

We long for our mothers to witness our fullest flowering, but sometimes the midsummer breeze augers something else entirely.

I was fortunate to be in Grace Paley's presence on a number of occasions. Three, in particular, I recall. One day in my early twenties, as a university student, I was offered a manuscript conference with her. She had read a story of mine, and we met so I could hear her advice. I was a melancholy kid. Why? I was a kid. She had nothing to offer regarding my manuscript. "Cheer up": that's all she said. Probably, it made me a better writer.

On the second occasion, a few years later, I saw her read at the Houston Museum of Fine Arts along with Toni Cade Bambara. Bambara was then writing about the Atlanta child murders, the controversies surrounding the mysterious deaths of several black boys in the city amid rumors of racism in the Atlanta Police Department. From the back of the room, a member of the audience shouted at Bambara, "This is a museum of art! It's not a forum for your damn politics!" Bambara was shaken and silenced, the crowd grew agitated. People stood and yelled at one another. Suddenly Grace, smacking gum, and wearing, I recall, bright red shoes, waddled to the podium, waved her hand, and said, "Sit down, sit down. Let me tell you a story." She told us a funny tale. I don't remember it now, but her humor and her calm defused the anger in the room. Once she'd made us happy, she lowered her voice. Quietly, firmly, she said: "Art can't be separated from politics." She invited Bambara back to the podium to finish her piece on the murders. No one objected.

The final occasion I recall occurred not long ago, though longer than I care to admit. Grace had come to Oregon to read to my writing students. She was staying in a rather prim B&B, in the shadow of large, leafy trees. In the evening, when my wife and I came to get her for dinner, we discovered she had not yet finished dressing. She stood in her room, at the window watching moonlight through the leaves, wearing a big, loose girdle. I swear, her swaying bosoms conjured the word "mother." She smiled at us, not the least bit embarrassed, and released a loud, lusty belch, a woman in the fullness of life, enjoying life to its fullest. How I miss her.

For all its grace, and occasional political punch, compression is a simple grammatical maneuver. Basic words. Basic units of expression. It thrives on coordinating conjunctions—*and, for, then, yet, so*; on dependent clauses, *although, despite*, allowing ideas to grow, to intertwine. Like cultivating a garden. The *But Moment* is often the key to a story, poem, or novel: what's left unsaid, implied but not stated? This is not just a question of discovering what lies beneath the surface. It's a matter of understanding what the surface, what the subject, what even the teller of a story, *absolutely cannot exist without. What pain makes barely articulable.*

So.

Then she died.

# The Tragic Necessity of Human Life

Grace Paley once said, "I don't have a story until I have two stories." She meant that one narrative line needs the countering force of another to give a story tension.

Willa Cather's version of Paley's dictum might read, "I don't have a story until I don't have a story."

At the center of Cather's 1925 novel, *My Mortal Enemy*, is a gap. In that gap the story occurs. Or doesn't. It is missing from the book.

"I first met Myra Henshawe when I was fifteen, but I had known about her ever since I could remember anything at all," explains our narrator, Nellie Birdseye. "She and her runaway marriage were the themes of the most interesting, indeed the only interesting, stories that were told in our family."

Tales of Myra's elopement with Oswald Henshawe enflame Nellie's romantic imagination. Myra sacrificed everything for love—or so Nellie is led to believe. Money, position in life: none of it mattered to Myra. Like a fairy tale creature, she fled with the man of her dreams, forsaking material comforts.

At one point, Nellie's aunt Lydia says she supposes Myra and Oswald have been as "happy as most people."

"That . . . was disheartening," Nellie responds. "The very point of their story was that they should be much happier than other people."

Nellie meets Myra in New York. She discovers that Myra's "account of her friends was often more interesting . . . than the people themselves." Reality pales before a good story.

But part 1 of *My Mortal Enemy* ends on a sour note. Aunt Lydia proclaims she is "sick of Myra's dramatics." "I've done with them," she says.

For reasons Nellie, with her bird's-eye view, can't fathom, not everyone considers Myra a princess.

Part 2 begins ten years later, clear across the continent, in a "sprawling overgrown west-coast city . . . stumbling all over itself and finally tumbl[ing] untidily into the sea." Nellie has arrived here because things have gone "badly" for her family (we get no details). She has taken a "position in a college—a college . . . as experimental and unsubstantial as everything else in this place." In its westward movement, America seems to have lost something essential.

By coincidence, Nellie encounters Myra and Oswald in the "wretchedly-built" apartment-hotel in which they have all rented rooms. Things have gone badly with the couple, as well. Myra is crippled, poor, and worse, she is bitter about the world and its peoples—"such pigs!" she says—and she is especially unhappy with Oswald, the major cause of her despair. She believes if she hadn't eloped with him, she wouldn't have wound up in this awful place.

Except: how *did* she wind up here?

That is the missing story.

What would seem to be the novel's focus—how a luscious romance became a life-and-death quarrel—remains in the gap, beyond Nellie's comprehension.

Some three years before writing *My Mortal Enemy*, Cather published an early version of her essay, "The Novel Démeublé." "The novel, for a long while, has been overfurnished," she says. She exhorts writers to strip their stories to the "play of emotions, great and little." "How wonderful it would be if we could throw all the furniture out the window, and along with it all the meaningless reiterations concerning physical sensations, all the tiresome old patterns, and leave the room as bare as the stage of a Greek theatre," she writes.

To help us imagine the ideal novel, she asks rhetorically, "Is the story of a banker who is unfaithful to his wife and who ruins himself by speculation in trying to gratify the caprices of his mistresses, at all reinforced by a masterly exposition of banking, our whole system of credits, the methods of the Stock Exchange?"

Well no, not necessarily—though Tom Wolfe would probably argue otherwise, waving in our faces a copy of *The Bonfire of the Vanities*.

But, granting Cather her point, it is hard not to feel that, in denuding *My Mortal Enemy*, presumably her first attempt at a novel démeublé, she has tossed the baby with the bathwater.

In part 1, we encounter Myra at a particular stage in her life. In part 2, we meet her at another stage, horribly changed. Absent drama, the novel offers no character development. Instead, we are presented with two situations. The sole link between these situations is Nellie's desire that Myra's story remain a fairy tale.

It hardly needs stating: real life is not a fairy tale. If demonstrating *that* was the purpose of Cather's novel, the effort wouldn't have been worth it.

Before the ten-year gap, one of our last glimpses of Myra comes at a New Year's Eve party. Myra entertains her New York friends, most of whom are "stage people." They are in a hurry to arrive at the party before the stroke of midnight (when magical spells break); many of them rush to Myra's apartment "with traces of [stage] make-up still on their faces." One man wears his "last-act wig" and carries "his plumed hat."

Nellie recalls the scene for us many years later, casting it in an amber glow. "Most of [those people] are dead now, but it was a fine group that stood around the table to drink the new year in," she says. "By far, the handsomest and most distinguished of the company was a woman no longer young but beautiful in age, Helena Modjeska. She looked a woman of another race and another period."

So: beneath the make-up and the masks lurk the faces of the dead. Madame Modjeska belongs to a different era, her youthful beauty a light in the fog. It's as though multiple time frames exist at once in this scene, like one silkscreen overlaid on another.

Crucially, what's missing is movement. Soon, part 1 will end. Early in part 2, it becomes clear that the story and the characters will not evolve. Instead, part 2 bleeds through into part 1. We are meant to accept that *Crippled* Myra has always existed in *Princess* Myra. Cather's interest lies not in change but in essence: "How wonderful it would be if we could . . . leave the room bare."

In *My Mortal Enemy*, she did not just discard the furniture, the bric-a-brac of chronology and plot. She exposed the plain surfaces of the walls so she could watch shadows dance across them—flat outlines of vague, fuller realities beyond.

In an essay written many years after the novel, but perhaps with the experience of the novel in mind, Cather said, "Nobody can paint the sun, or sunlight. [The artist] can only paint the tricks that shadows play with it, or what it does to forms."

The image recalls Plato's famous Allegory of the Cave, his assertion that ideal forms (of beings and things) exist in the cosmos beyond our ken. Here on Earth, we see only the imperfect shades they cast. Our lives are flawed parodies of the forms' immortal movements and shapes.

The *story* of a life, its duration and formal evolution, is a wisp. Cather was after the essence. "Whatever is felt upon the page without being specifically named there—that, we may say, is created," she says.

In *My Mortal Enemy*, the ideal principle driving Myra's life would seem to be romance. In fact, it turns out to be something more twisted, a "violent nature" seeking one distraction, one form of salvation after another. In its violence, it exhausts what it seeks, betraying itself. Romance is *Nellie's* essence, not Myra's.

The gap in the center of the novel is necessary to convey that time and events affect Myra's nature not at all. Her *story*, the "tiresome old patterns," is of little consequence. What matters is the *overlay* and what it reveals. Only by seeing every Myra at once—to the extent that narrative linearity allows—can we grasp the core of her being.

Cather once said, "Human relationships are the tragic necessity of human life.... [T]hey can never be wholly satisfactory.... [E]very ego is half the time greedily seeking them, and half the time pulling away from them." A tiresome old pattern, indeed, if that's your view of mortal affairs. The *stuff* of traditional stories, daily habits, the furniture in the rooms where we make and break our habits, failed to engage Willa Cather. Her gaze was somewhere else.

In another essay, she spoke of an exhibition of old and modern Dutch paintings she saw once in Paris. "In many of them, the scene presented was a living room warmly furnished, or a kitchen full of food and coppers," she wrote. "But in most of the interiors, whether dining-room or kitchen, there was a square window open, through which one saw the masts of the ships or a stretch of gray sea. The feeling of the sea that one got through those square windows was remarkable."

Foreground and background, completing the perspective. Once again, we encounter a cave-like space, a sheltering place for contrasting transient movements (preparing, consuming the food), with a vaster, more lasting vision beyond.

Refuge and prospect.


At the end of *My Mortal Enemy,* Myra asks that after her death her ashes be scattered "in some lonely and unfrequented place . . . or in the sea."

The fleeting: cast upon the endlessly borne, the endlessly repeating.

Cather's novelistic gaze was toward the eternal, seeking the abiding essences beyond our crabbily furnished little rooms, where we enact, upon and with each other, our tragic necessities.

# Perhaps America

*An Homage to Sherwood Anderson*

Sherwood Anderson was an American storyteller who wanted to be an artist. The myth of the artist was strong in him. Late one afternoon, in the fall of 1912, he told a secretary in his Elyria, Ohio, ad agency, "My feet are cold and wet. I have been walking too long on the bed of a river," and left his office, never to return. He was thirty-six years old. Thirty years later, he described the incident as a rejection of money, a commitment to the art of writing. He'd forgotten how mentally exhausted he was, so he invented a story to explain his illness.

After leaving the office, he wandered for three days, scribbling nonsense in a notebook, without a clue as to who he was. He was attracted to the kitchen lights in the houses on the outskirts of town, but when he tried to approach them, dogs chased him away. On the second day he saw a woman hanging dresses on a line. He wanted to go to her but a collie kept watch at her feet. The woman was beautiful. He had always been a little afraid of beautiful women. He didn't know why. It seemed he was always attracted to what he couldn't have.

He might have explained it this way: you're longing, let's say, for a woman. If you imagine another man caressing her shoulders, or if, alone at night, you remember the delicate hair on her arms, you ache and there's nothing for it but whiskey, sleep, or travel. Loss and all the distance within it was in Sherwood Anderson's gaze that day as the woman unfolded her wet slips and dresses.

Twenty-four hours later he awoke in a Cleveland hospital. He was haggard and groggy. He didn't want to see his colleagues or his wife. While doctors and nurses fussed over his physical condition—he was sunburned and dehydrated—he worried over larger matters. It was all so confusing, this struggle for money and sex. Work and marriage were supposed to ease these longings, but they didn't, not for anyone he knew, though everyone pretended to be happy.

Lying in his hospital bed, wondering how he'd got there, he decided to be honest with himself. He couldn't give freely to his wife. He was, perhaps, a little afraid of the sexual power he saw in her, though what that power was he couldn't say. He was a skilled writer but he was using his talents to sell products he didn't believe in. At night, in secret, he had written a few small stories about his hometown, but he was too shy to show them to anyone. Now, flat on his back, he cursed his timidity. He knew he couldn't return to his family and his job. It was time to test himself and his stories. If he didn't try to succeed as a writer, he'd always wonder what might have been.

When he recovered from his illness, he untangled himself from the obligations of his old identity. He moved to Chicago, a literary capital. He'd heard about parties there where writers and painters wore chic, outrageous clothes: zoot-suits, waist-length strings of pearls. They talked about modernism, rhyme schemes, socialism. He bought a funny hat—well, but it was chic, wasn't it? He hoped to scope out these sophisticated affairs and perhaps be introduced to an editor who might publish his stories.

"I support the working men and women in their struggle against the monopolies!" someone shouted one night at a party Anderson managed to attend by pretending to know someone who knew someone.

"Yes, but the working men and women know nothing of art!"

"Do you suppose the president has read Zola?"

"Honey! The president thinks Zola's a river in Africa!"

Anderson pressed against a wall, crushing the brim of his hat. These people had read so much more than he had. They were so much more experienced with politics. He would have to learn to scorn the president. He would have to—

"Do you paint or do you write?" The woman who'd asked him this didn't really care. That was clear. She was looking for a place to sit against the wall, to rest her feet from all the dancing. She was making small talk to be polite. She hitched up her pearls—they hung past her knees—and smiled. He smoothed his hat. Her question gave him a chance to launch his new identity. Weeks later, he began to be welcomed at the parties. His face became familiar around town—it helped that he'd thrown away the hat. All he'd had to do was say he was a writer. It was simple! No one questioned him. No one ever really talked about their work. No one offered to read what he wrote . . . until one night the editor of a small quarterly asked to see a piece or two. After passing him some stories, Anderson spent a week biting his nails, pacing his room. The following Saturday, he went to another gathering. The editor was there but he spent most of the evening avoiding Anderson. Anderson knew his stories had been a failure. He looked for the woman with the pearls. He didn't see her. Finally, as everyone was leaving, hailing cabs on the street and calling goodbye, the editor walked up and put his arm on Anderson's shoulder. Apparently, alcohol had emboldened him. "Your pieces are cute," he said, "especially the ones about adolescence. But they're not polished or refined. They aren't really art. Read Turgenev. Read Lawrence. Read Mark Twain. They'll show you how a writer makes a story."

In the weeks ahead, it became a refrain among the Chicago artists: Sherwood Anderson would never write a novel. They said this though most of them had never read him. Still, they insisted, it was common knowledge. A major achievement wasn't in him. He had simply come to writing too late.

For many years afterward he traveled restlessly, freelancing, working here and there as a newspaper editor. At the age of forty-nine he wrote a novel called *Dark Laughter*. Mark Twain's stories about the Mississippi River were fresh in his mind, and he wrote, like Twain, of shiftless fathers and lazy lives. He wanted to make great fiction but he worried: maybe he'd thought about it too much, tried too hard? Maybe it wasn't very good.

Vague sentences run like broken fences through the novel. Near the beginning, the narrator asks himself, "What was a fellow to do?" Sadly, he never finds out. Neither does the reader. The book tells the stories of the "Negroes" who lived along the Mississippi River in the 1920s.

They know, as white Americans do not, how to experience the highest possibilities in life, and they laugh at the whites' neurotic affairs. They never complain about their poverty. The novel's middle-class heroine enjoys nice dresses and trips to Paris but winds up running away with a laborer who's lost his job. Overnight, she abandons her ideals. Besides failing to mend these narrative gaffes, Anderson hurls stones at Mark Twain's achievement: "He might have written of song killed, of men herded into a new age of speed, of factories, of swift, fast-running trains. Instead he wrote stale jokes."

Anderson wanted to gather what he'd heard, felt, and thought on the river. He tried to make great fiction when he wrote *Dark Laughter*. In Chicago, at the parties-till-dawn, folks said it wasn't a very good book. It wasn't much like art.

In another book, a sprawling and muddled work called *Many Marriages*, Anderson wrote, "Love-making was after all a symbol of something more filled with meaning than the mere act of two bodies embracing, the passage of the seeds of life from one body to another." Somehow, he had got it into his head that symbolism was a sure sign of art in a book. He thought it made great fiction. Ivan Turgenev, the great Russian writer whom he'd learned to admire, used symbolism to sharpen his social criticism. Mark Twain used it to enhance his Mississippi River settings—the water as border between the future and the past, one world and another. That sort of thing. Anderson grew self-conscious writing *Dark Laughter* and *Many Marriages* because he wanted to do what Turgenev and Twain did with symbols. It was beginning to look as though the Chicago artists were right. Sherwood Anderson couldn't write a novel.

He had, however, written *Winesburg, Ohio*, a book of stories modestly successful with readers in Paris, if not in Chicago, and he'd written a story called "The Egg." "The Egg" is a cleanly made story about a man who tries to force an egg into a bottle to entertain a customer in his restaurant. Well. The egg won't fit into the bottle. The customer laughs at him. The man grows enraged. Upstairs, his wife and son try to sleep.

When the customer leaves, the restaurant owner lumbers up the stairs and, gripping the egg, kneels beside his wife's bed. The egg has defeated him. The boy, who of course couldn't sleep that night, tells the story. A gloomy man now, he reminisces about his past. He remembers his father's exhaustion. "As to what happened downstairs," he says, "for some unexplainable reason, I know the story as well as though I had been a witness to my father's discomfiture. One in time gets to know many unexplainable things." He'd lain in bed, you see, wanting to sleep. He couldn't have known what his father was doing to entertain the customer, but he *does* know. Perhaps his father told him later what happened. Perhaps he made it up. In any case, he tells the story, rediscovering as he does so the crucial event of his life. "I wondered why eggs had to be. The question got into my blood. It has stayed there, I imagine, because I am the son of my father." The egg defeated him too, you see. He developed a gloomy temperament.

Anderson wrote another story, "The Man Who Became a Woman." It is like "The Egg": short, simple sentences make the story clean. The narrator stops in the middle to explain, "I'm just trying to make you understand some things about me, as I would like to understand some things about you, or anyone, if I had the chance."

The writing gropes, clambers forward unevenly, but the tone is true, unburdened by symbols. The teller, a naïve man, chisels in the dark, slipping into his back pocket large, sparkling pieces of knowledge about his fellow human beings.

Anderson's best stories came to him like brief, charming moments in an otherwise difficult life: watching a happy boy gallop like a horse, or coming upon an old couple casting seeds across a field in the middle of the night. His talent was for rendering quick impressions. Later in life, he came to believe that storytellers were nothing more than scribblers. They weren't ambitious enough. *Puzzled America*, one of his books about poverty during the Great Depression, asks, Can anyone who doesn't respect the ground beneath his feet make a claim to aristocracy? But in a way, it seems, *he* wanted to be an aristocrat, an artist. The problem was, he let the ground dry up, the stories, the base on which he stood.

Perhaps it had something to do with America, with the artists he'd met. They impressed him with their fashionable talk and their chic new clothes. They seemed to know the secrets of life, while storytellers appeared to be simpler folk, pacing their rooms in confusion, wringing moments out of their heads, slinging ink across a page.

Or it may be that a different kind of ambition got into him. On a trip to Paris he met Gertrude Stein. He had read her "rose is a rose is a rose" and he talked to her about art and writing. He said of her later, "Miss Stein is a worker in words with the same loving touch in her strong fingers that was characteristic of the women of the kitchens of the brick houses in the town of my boyhood. In her own great kitchen she is making something with her materials, something sweet and fragrant."

She convinced Anderson he was one of the few men in America who could write a sentence. Well. She thought he had something—an ear for language, perhaps. The people at the parties in Chicago sure didn't have it, she said.

He respected Gertrude Stein and thought she was an artist. It may be that he began to pay more attention to individual words and phrases than to the shapes of his stories. He wanted to be an artist too, you see, only he was a storyteller and he couldn't write like Gertrude Stein or the folks at the parties, and now I'm writing this, I suppose, because I'm a little sad that he wanted so badly to be one of them. I'm trying to get at something in the man. I don't know if I can.

He kept a notebook. In the notebook there is not much talk of being an artist. He writes:

Consider the tantalizing difference in the quality of work produced by two men. In the first we get at times an almost overwhelming sense of proficiency in his craft. The writer, we feel, knows form, knows construction, knows words. How he slings words about. Almost every one of his lines is quotable.

And this other fellow. His words do not cling, his art forms become at times shapeless, he stumbles, going crudely and awkwardly forward.

And how breathlessly we follow. What is he doing that he holds us so tightly? What is the secret of our love of him, even in the midst of his awkwardness? He is revealing himself to us. See how shamelessly and boldly he is trying.

The notebook's fragments say it's fine to tell stories, unpolished or no. Anderson himself could be the awkward writer referenced here. The crafted writer is perhaps Gertrude Stein or Ernest Hemingway, one of her protégés. At one time he was a student of Anderson's, too. Hemingway displayed an overwhelming knowledge of form, construction, words. When he wasn't writing he hunted and fished or watched men slaughter bulls. The myth of the man was strong in him. He wanted to be powerful and alone like the American men in his stories. Rivers slice through his books, and mountains so sharp you think you'll bloody your fingers flipping the pages, and there are men in those rivers, American men fighting fish, and men clinging to rocks in the smoke of war, and they're powerful and alone, and I suppose I'm a little sad that he wanted so badly to be a man. No one can be powerful and alone all the time. Ernest Hemingway, an American man, shot himself in the head because he couldn't keep living like the men in his stories.

No one can be a man all the time. Sherwood Anderson understood this. "The Man Who Became a Woman" is a story about that. In it, a lonely boy lives by a racetrack, currycombing horses, feeding them and walking them in the mornings. He pats their handsome faces and wishes they were women strolling beside him. He loves a young man, Tom Means, for his kindness and ambition. Tom wants to write about what it's like to be a racehorse swipe.

One night a couple of black boys, workers around the track, nearly rape the boy in the hayloft where he sleeps. In the moonlight they mistake him for a woman. He runs naked into muddy fields, followed by the laughter of the Negroes. Several yards from the track, he falls into the carcass of a horse. The chalky ribs grip his arms, mud sucks at his feet and legs.

Grown now, he narrates the story. He's embarrassed about that night. He'd been lonely, you see, wanting a woman, loving Tom and respecting him. His friends, the other racehorse swipes, walked into town on the weekends to drink and shout and dance with the local girls. He always stayed behind to watch the horses. That night he fell asleep in the hay.

Something was bothering him. Earlier that evening he had seen his face in a smoky mirror and it looked to him like the face of a girl. Afterward, the boys mistook him for a woman. There was his love for Tom Means.

Well. He didn't know what to think.

Years later, telling the story, he's no longer so rattled by those particular events, but you can tell he's uneasy and puzzled about something. "I'm not any fairy," he claims. "Anyone who has ever known me knows better than that." But the thing is, you can tell he's bothered. He wouldn't say this if he weren't.

Tom Means never wrote about horses or men. Something defeated him down the road, the way the egg defeated the restaurant owner and his son. Gloomy men, eh, men who fail? Sherwood Anderson knew about that. He was a storyteller who wanted to be an artist.

"The Man Who Became a Woman" depends on the unevenness of the writing for its success as a story. The man is trying to get at something. It's hard for him, and his stumbling reveals that. In the story, black laughter rises high as crows in the middle of the night, like the laughter of the Negroes on the mud flats near the Mississippi River. While the whites turn gloomy, the blacks do their work, enjoy themselves, and laugh as smoothly as river water washing over polished stones. Then the story plummets into sexual confusion, the way a shot bird falls into a canyon.

At his best, Anderson turned puzzlement into a procedure. He knew that a man can't be a man all the time, powerful and alone. He wanted to understand what life was like for different kinds of men. "American men cannot understand love between man and man," he once wrote his son John. "If you have such experiences in life as I have had, I think you will find that finding a few real companions is the most difficult thing on earth. You will have to take what you can get here and there. It is a great mistake to draw away too much."

"The Mississippi River drives me to despair," he wrote. "I go to it every day, spend hours walking beside it. I get on boats and travel up and down the river. Writing should flow toward its inevitable end as majestically and powerfully as the great river flows down to the Gulf." His private struggle with art and with Mark Twain's river becomes, in his novels, the struggle of American whites to set themselves in motion, to give themselves over to the motion of the river and the blood. But the structures of his novels couldn't support the flowing power he wanted to get into them. He couldn't sustain a simple story of rediscovery like "The Egg" or "The Man Who Became a Woman." Imagine how hard it would be to write an entire novel in one sitting while the wet snow pelted your window and your fellow lodgers banged on your door, wanting to come in.

In the long form, he wasn't content to ponder over people. He wanted to be visionary. Symbolic. "There was a cleansing, a strange sort of renewal within the house of the man or woman when the god Life came in," he writes in *Many Marriages*, hoping to encircle his characters with a vision as sturdy as a chain link fence.

In his visionary mood, he liked to think the idea for *Dark Laughter* came to him in a flash one day as he was going to clean his house. At the time he was working as an advertising writer and making a pretty fair living. That afternoon, he said, his black maid chuckled at his clumsy preparations. "'Oh,' I thought. 'If some white woman, who might conceivably love me, would be willing to live with me, would be willing to take the attitude toward me this Negro woman now took.' It was from her that I got the impulse for *Dark Laughter*."

In fact, a series of letters written in 1922, three years before the novel was published, show that Anderson had been trying for a long time to understand something about black people. The idea for *Dark Laughter* didn't occur to him in an afternoon. It grew on him during subsequent trips to New Orleans.

A couple of Chicago artists, Lucile and Jerry Blum, received his letters, the first dated January 1922. Soon to complete *Many Marriages*, Anderson traveled to New Orleans to relax in the hyacinth courtyards and stroll through the Mardi Gras museums. He told his friends there were "plenty of niggers" in New Orleans—the only mention of black folks in the letter. He hadn't yet taken much of an interest in the people. When he had been some months away from the city, he began to value the Vieux Carré and its lifestyle. He wrote the Blums in March of that year, "New Orleans got me hard, the place, the people, and everything.

Some day I'll tell you more about it. New York and Chicago are like tense, closed fists. New Orleans is an open-handed place."

His next letter, dated November 1922, comes from New Orleans. He had, let us say, spent the day walking among the monuments in a massive old cemetery. White marble chilled his hands as he felt the chiseled dates in the stones. Late in the afternoon he wandered toward the riverfront, pausing to watch the tugboats labor toward Saint Louis. After dinner he settled into a wrought iron chair beneath an orange canopy and sipped a green, tangy drink. Across a narrow alley a woman swept her kitchen porch. He scribbled in a notebook phrases heard on the river. Workers unloading boats yelled at one another. White workers, black workers. He wanted to remember their oaths, their tired grunts. He might use them in a story. Then he began the letter: "The nigger thing comes back strong. I've seen some things here that are illuminating, but I will talk to you about them rather than write. The thing would be to live and work in town but to have a Ford and go out into the smaller nigger towns. It isn't so much that we write of the nigger, paint the nigger, but that we get their abandonment of feeling, their rhythmic sense of life, skies, the river here. Everything at moments seems in them, and they in it all. Do I make myself clear?"

Naïve, yes. Stereotyped. Romantic. Unintentionally racist. But at least, you see, he had begun to try to understand a different way of life in America. Ernest Hemingway, his protégé, powerful and alone, understood only one kind of life for American men. Perhaps he never really puzzled over people the way Sherwood Anderson did. Anderson wrote stories to teach himself the truth . . . then the ground dried up. He worked a poor farm.

"I would like to write the story of a man during an hour of his life, without physical action, the man sitting or standing or just walking about. All that he is that makes him what he is." Why couldn't he be content with that? While dancing, some of the artists at the parties in Chicago would whisper about him: maybe he'd injured his imagination somewhere on one of his many travels to Louisiana or Ohio or on a steamer to Paris.

Me—I want to suggest it wasn't entirely his fault, that perhaps it had something to do with America.

He explains at the beginning of his Depression essays, "I am in the position of many writers nowadays. Formerly, for a good many years, I was a writer of tales. It may be I should have remained just that, but there is a difficulty. There are, everywhere in America, these people now out of work."

Blacks, whites, others were starving. Children labored in factories without any pay. Against all this, his stories felt like trifles. A well-made sentence couldn't feed a man. If he had stayed in Paris like Gertrude Stein he might have continued to write cleanly without the sight of so many poor miners and railroad workers troubling his storytelling, but then he would be fleeing his country's problems. He had run away, before, to become a writer of tales. He wasn't running any more.

America is hard on writers who stumble. Anderson wrote a few weak books like *Dark Laughter* and *Many Marriages*, and America became impatient with him. Critics trounced him and his work. They said he was sex-obsessed and that he stole his style from Turgenev. They called him the phallic Chekhov.

Then, conscience-stricken, he began documenting the lives of miners and mill workers. The 1930s produced some of his best work, as in this snapshot of mill girls:

> In the mill [Doris] and Grace worked in the same big light long spinning-room between the rows of bobbins. They ran up and down or walked up and down or stopped a minute to talk. When you work with some one that way all day every day, you can't help getting to like her. You get to love her. It's like being married almost. You know when she is tired because you are tired. If your feet ache you know hers do. You can't tell, just walking through a place and seeing people working, like Doris and Grace did. You don't know. You don't feel it.

For literary critics, sentimentality was the great sin. They were so alert to sentimentality they sometimes confused genuine sentiment for it. For his mill portraits, Anderson was dismissed by many critics as a muckraker, a mere journalist, a dupe of the Communist Party. The Chicago artists ignored him. They fawned over William Faulkner and other newcomers. Instead of acknowledging Anderson with the sensitivity they claimed to possess in abundance, they treated him as though he were a retired office clerk deserving nothing more than an inexpensive gold watch. They forgot stories like "The Egg" and "The Man Who Became a Woman." Stories about America. Clean stories. Art.

So his native land lost interest in Sherwood Anderson. Finding a few real companions is the most difficult thing on earth, eh?

One day he boarded an ocean liner for South America. At dinner on peaceful waters off the coast of Panama he swallowed a toothpick, and it punctured his intestines: a brief moment like one of his stories that cost him his life.

Had he lived longer, he would have been disappointed but not surprised by the death of Ernest Hemingway, who never understood that a man can't be a man all the time (*he had so much equipment on*); disappointed but not surprised by the deterioration of America's cities, and the men and women still out of work; disappointed by Gertrude Stein's lack of readership ("I have always listened to the way everybody has to tell what they have to say").

"You see, the writer wants to explain himself," Anderson wrote in his notebook. "He is a lover and so vividly does he love that he has the courage to love even himself. And so it is the lover who sits writing and the madness of the writer is the madness of the lover. When he writes he is making love. Surely all can understand that?"

He would have been disappointed by the small number of people who understand that. Well. Perhaps it's a little romantic. Perhaps there's no place in America for romance of that sort. I'm a little sad if that's true. I'm a little sad now that I've written this. I wanted to get at something in the man. I don't know if I did.

# Afterword

*Let Us Build Us a City*

Samuel Beckett once taped to the wall above his desk in Paris a slip of paper with an appeal on it to help him through his writing days. It said, "Fail. Fail again. Fail better."

And that was Beckett at his most optimistic. In a darker mood he wrote, "Nothing to paint. Nothing to paint with." Donald Barthelme, Beckett's most faithful American disciple, echoed the Irishman's uncertainty. "What an artist does is fail," he said, adding that "not-knowing"— at best having a "slender intuition"—is "crucial to art, is what permits art to be made."

I offer these somber assessments of work not to end this volume on a discouraging note but to suggest the mystery and power of creating new worlds, which is precisely what poets and storytellers do, and it is what teachers and students embark upon whenever they gather to build a community. Just as a page holds nothing before we mark it with words, a setting, a place, an institution, a town, can be spiritually empty without enormous cooperative and creative effort. "Let us build us a city!" says the Book of Genesis, and the mystery and power behind that simple statement rests in the implication that out of nothing will come—somehow, gloriously—something.

Back to that blank piece of paper: say you draw a line on it, the beginning of your favorite word. If the paper is waxy, your pen may slip. If it's lightly wrinkled, your line will skitter off-center. Noting all this, a scientist might say *blankness* has properties that affect *what is*. Beckett and Barthelme would argue, after Shakespeare, that *nothing* determines the kind of *something* we get. Here's Leontes, from Shakespeare's *The Winter's Tale*:

Is whispering nothing?
Is leaning cheek to cheek? is meeting noses? ... Skulking in corners? Wishing
clocks more swift?
Hours, minutes? noon, midnight? ...
Why then the world, and all that's in't, is nothing,
The covering sky is nothing ...
If this be nothing.

From the slenderest provocations—whispers, little nothings in the
ear, the thick ticking of a tin clock—worlds are built. Nothing, or as
near to nothing as human affairs can get, is something after all.

In the beginning, says the old story, the earth was without form and
void. Then language asserted its power: "Let there be light!" Now we are
able to sit together in classrooms or in book groups, if we choose, discussing literature; we are able to attend readings and lectures, soaked
in warm illumination from state-of-the-art ceiling fixtures. We have
someone to pay the electric bills, to keep the lights burning. We have
shelter, a viable infrastructure, all founded, if you believe the story, on
a single sentence, a grouping of words so light as to be nearly nothing:
miraculously, mysteriously, we have built a city.

But these places will be uninspired unless we animate them by
turning our whispering, our wishing, our narratives into a communal
*something*. Even when we find a circle of like-minded folks, we have no
guarantees that the world we've entered will succeed. I'm not speaking
here of the tangibles—budgets, publicity, logistical support—though
those are crucial to any formal or informal organization of people.
I'm thinking of the intangibles invisible to surveys and productivity
charts, but that will ultimately determine the kind of something we get.
Personal chemistry. Cooperation. Generosity. Imagination.

What an artist does is fail? Communities fail, too, daily. Inevitably,
they fail to meet our expectations. Tensions mar them. Glitches. They
are vulnerable to hazy planning, bad timing, unforeseen circumstances.
Entering any institution, or informal alliance, we invite all sorts of
risk. Will we be generous enough, cooperative enough, imaginative
enough to overcome our frustrations with bureaucratic burdens, insuf-
ficient resources, and one another to fail and fail again, better, more

productively, until from our faltering comes whatever we agree to call success?

Wherever we find community—in a brick-and-mortar institution, online, among sympathetic reader-friends, or by holding a book such as this in our hands—we are fortunate to be accompanied by invisible comrades, only a few of whose names I've invoked: Beckett, Barthelme, Shakespeare, Bernard Malamud ("the thick ticking of the tin clock" comes from his story, "Idiots First"). Ghosts circle us—whispering absences, carrying on with us the world's literary conversation. And our personal ghosts travel with us, too, losses and failures that often support our boldest stories and poems.

Let's face it: many of us turn to writing *because* of failure. The world has failed to satisfy us, so we want to revise it. Our revisions have let us down, so we hope to improve them. Our family's demands, our peers' pressures, have left us unfulfilled, so we've thrown ourselves at the mercy of a slender intuition, scratching out our little stories.

No one can foresee the somethings we'll create out of our experiences in any place we land. We can only hope to fail better, not worse.

Ultimately, only the individual can determine what her talent is, what will nurture it best, how and where to take it. An institution, *any* establishment, offers time, structure, and companionship to help us clarify these things. It offers appeals to get us through our writing days. On such slender assurances, worlds are built.

Already, we know that nothing may come of our efforts. Our best work may wind up skulking in corners. In part, that uncertainty—the need to face it—is what got us to this point. And I want to encourage us to see this not-knowing as one of our strongest assets. Like light, anxiety is a fine source of energy, failure a robust motivator.

One last somber counsel: it's the useless we're chasing, the intuitions and emotions, beyond the practical, that nearly elude our words— whatever is, for each of us, sublime. These things sustain us, abide with us, but cannot be put to firm use. Whatever is used routinely, merely to fill a function, is soon faded, worn, broken. Art does something else.

Thinking about baseball, William Carlos Williams wrote:

The crowd at the ball game
is moved uniformly

by a spirit of uselessness
which delights them

all the exciting details
of the chase

and the escape, the error
the flash of genius

all to no end save beauty
the eternal

To find the delights in uselessness, the somethings in nothing—that's why we gather with only the slightest notion of what might happen, to build communities of thinkers, readers, writers. That's why we fill empty pages, to risk the mystery and power of creating new worlds, which can explode in every word. In his first short stanza, Williams offers us the useless delight of a pun: the word "uniformly," noting both the crowd's solidarity, and the visual spectacle of uniformed men on the field. And the final lines: eternity, of course, has no end, but "no end" also means, in Williams's context, "no purpose." The word "save" does double-duty here, whispering both "salvation" and "exception."

Stripping things to the near-nothing of their strictest essence, their first principles. No end to no purpose. These were the hallmarks of Williams's art, from which we all can learn. They are the kinds of things we *hope* to learn by reading and by studying writing, the lessons on which we build a creative and imaginatively generous society.

# ACKNOWLEDGMENTS

Portions of this book appeared originally, in different forms, in the following publications: *The Writers Chronicle, Standpoints, The Georgia Review, The Crab Orchard Review, The Los Angeles Review of Books, Gulf Coast,* and *Oregon Humanities.* I am grateful to the editors of these publications for permission to reprint.

I am indebted to the following people for offering initial opportunities to air some of the ideas in this book, formally or informally: Pete Turchi, Ellen Bryant Voigt, Stephen Corey, Kathleen Holt, David Fenza, Ellen Meeropol, and my students and colleagues at Oregon State University. Kathryn Lang, Michael Homler, Kit Ward, and Colleen Mohyde kept the possibilities alive. For their friendship and good counsel, my thanks to David and Lindsay Huddle, Kevin and Amy Clark, Dinah Lenney and Fred Mills, Ted Leeson and Betty Campbell, Michelle Boisseau and Tom Stroik, David Turkel and Elena Passarello, Sue and Larry Rodgers, Keith Scribner and Jen Richter, Karen Holmberg and Aria Minu-Sepehr, Jon and Martha Lewis, Debra and Creighton Lindsay, Kris and Rich Daniels, Bob and Mary Jo Nye, George Estreich, David Biespiel, Suzanne Berne, Molly Brown, Martha Low, Jon Ross, Jay Clarke, Lane Millet, Scott Nadelson, Glenn Blake, and Rosellen Brown. Candles for my ghosts: Gene and JoAnne Daugherty, Jeanne Sandor, George Manner, Jack Myers, Donald Barthelme, Tim Steele, and Ehud Havazelet. For Hannah Crum, Joey and Charlie Vetter, and Debra Daugherty: hope. At the University of Georgia Press, Elizabeth Crowley, John Joerschke, and Lisa M. Bayer graced the manuscript with careful attention. John Domini gave it a close and helpful reading. Sue Breckenridge copyedited the manuscript with graceful expertise. John Griswold offered keen insight and stronger support than I had any right to expect—very special thanks to him. Finally, to my wife and literary partner, Marjorie Sandor, abiding love and gratitude. *Tenemos.*

# NOTES

## Introduction

1   *"great disgrace and danger"*: Dante, *The Banquet of Dante Alighieri: Il Convivio*, trans. Elizabeth Price Sayer (London: George Routledge and Sons, 1887), 15.

3   *"he seemed to be his own number one groupie"*: Susan Cheever, *Home before Dark* (Boston: Houghton Mifflin Company, 1984), 210.

6   *Jay Martin notes*: Jay Martin, *Harvests of Change: American Literature 1865–1914* (Englewood Cliffs, N.J.: Prentice Hall, 1967), 16–21.

7   *Their novels are not*: Hugh Kenner, *A Homemade World: The American Modernist Writers* (New York: Alfred A. Knopf, 1975), 3.

7   *"wonder and awe"*: Philip Roth, "Writing American Fiction," in *Reading Myself and Others* (New York: Farrar, Straus & Giroux, 1975), 121.

8   *"There is a lake"*: Gerald of Wales, *The Topography of Ireland, The History of the Conquest of Ireland*, trans. Thomas Wright (London: George Bob, 1900). See also Malcolm Chapman, "Gerald of Wales," in *The Celts: The Construction of a Myth* (New York: St. Martin's Press, 1992), 185–200.

9   *"panther whose fragrance"*: Dante Alighieri, *De vulgari eloquentia*, trans. Warman Welliver (Chapel Hill: University of North Carolina Press, 1981), 71.

9   *"places and the people in them"*: William Gass, "The Medium of Fiction," in *Fiction and the Figures of Life* (New York: Alfred A. Knopf, 1970), 27.

9   *"She continued to walk"*: Henry James, *The Golden Bowl*, vol. 2 (New York: Charles Scribner and Sons, 1909), 236.

## Old Haunts

14   *"We had lots of jokes"*: Laurie Winslow, "Blood Puddles outside Building," *Tulsaworld.com*, February 8, 2000.

14   *"government at all levels"*: Tulsa Race Riot Commission, preliminary report submitted to Governor Frank Keating of Oklahoma on February 7, 2000.

15   *"in real and tangible form"*: ibid.

15   *"People are going to say"*: Randy Kreihbiel, "Panel Recommends Race Riot Reparations," *Tulsaworld.com*, November 23, 1999.

15   *Abe Deutschendorf*: ibid.

16   *"Whatever happened to the American past?"*: Sven Birkerts, *Readings* (Saint Paul, Minn.: Graywolf Press, 1999), 23–24.

17   *"hog squeal of the universe"*: Upton Sinclair, *The Jungle* (New York: Bantam, 1981), 15.

17   *"connect a bygone time"*: Nathaniel Hawthorne, preface to *The House of Seven Gables* (Boston: Houghton Mifflin Company, 1952), 13–15.

18   *"wrong-doing of one generation"*: ibid.

18   *"Its whole visible exterior"*: Hawthorne, *The House of Seven Gables*, 17, 24–25.

19   *"blood upon her white robes"*: Edgar Allan Poe, "The Fall of the House of Usher," in *The Complete Stories of Edgar Allan Poe* (New York: Vintage, 1975), 245.

19   *"very trifling and very temporary variation"*: ibid., 232.

20   *"Form ever follows function"*: Louis H. Sullivan, "The Tall Office Building Artistically Considered," *Lippincott's Magazine*, March 1896, 408.

21   *"finger-pointing fiction"*: Albert Murray, *The Hero and the Blues* (New York: Vintage Books, 1973), 45.

21   *"Why is it"*: ibid., 46.

21   *"social conscience"*: ibid., 46, 55.

22   *"about how life"*: Grace Paley, "Wants," in *The Collected Stories* (New York: Farrar, Straus, & Giroux, 1994), 130.

22   *"decayed wooden warehouses"* and subsequent quotes in this section: Nathaniel Hawthorne, "The Custom House: Introductory to *The Scarlet Letter*," in *The Scarlet Letter* (New York: Harcourt, Brace, and World, 1961), 3–5, 16–18.

24   *"whole range of human motivation"*: Murray, *The Hero and the Blues*, 49.

24   *"New ideas must come from old buildings"*: Jane Jacobs, *The Death and Life of Great American Cities* (New York: Random House, 1961), 245.

24   *"How much of old material"*: Hawthorne, *The House of Seven Gables*, 18.

25   *"After discussion . . . [a] bill was introduced"*: Tulsa Race Riot Commission, http://www.ok-history.mus.ok.us/trc/nov14.htm.

26   *"with the development of conscious, articulate citizens"*: Ralph Ellison, introduction to *Invisible Man*, in *The Collected Essays of Ralph Ellison*, ed. John F. Callahan (New York: The Modern Library, 1995), 482.

27   *"Kinney, is the world on fire?"*: Brent Staples, "Unearthing a Riot," *New York Times Magazine*, December 19, 1999, 64.

27   *"I thought I knew history"*: Buck Wolf, "Unearthing Ugly History," television feature, at *ABCNews.com* (1999).

27   *"Nobody knows what happened to him"*: ibid.

27   *"few hundred to several thousand"*: Brief for Plaintiff in Error, *Redfearn v. American Century Insurance Company*, 243 P 929 (Okla. 1926).

27   *"There was a long tumultuous shouting sound"*: Poe, "The Fall of the House of Usher," 245.

27   *"As a novelist I invented characters"*: Jewell Parker Rhodes, *Magic City* (New York: HarperCollins, 1997), 270.

28   *"on the ash-muddied ground"*: Susan Straight, *The Gettin Place* (New York: Hyperion Books, 1996), 318.

29   *"stripped of all [his] history"*: William Goyen, *The House of Breath* (New York: Persea Books, 1986), 1–3, 9, 14, 19, 24.

30   *"It seemed that the house was built"*: ibid., 193–94.

30   *"past whose annihilation had not taken place"*: Gabriel García Márquez, *One Hundred Years of Solitude*, trans. Gregory Rabassa (New York: Avon Books, 1971), 408–9.

31   *"showed [him] the way"*: Gabriel García Márquez, cited in Nick Sheerin, "Juan Rulfo's Only Novel Is . . .," in *Serpent's Tail* blog, September 18, 2014, https://serpentstail.com/blog/juan-rulfos-only-novel-is/.

31   *"walls stained red by the setting sun"*: Juan Rulfo, *Pedro Páramo* (New York: Grove Press, 1994), 7.

31   *"everyone [went] away as braceros"*: Juan Rulfo, *Inframundo* (Mexico City: Ediciones del Norte, 1983), 16.

31   *Even the Washington, D.C., home of the Environmental Protection Agency*: see the National Federation of Federal Employees Local 2050, "Indoor Air Quality and Work Environment Study: Environmental Protection Agency Headquarters," supplement to volume 1, "Employee Adverse Health Effects Information," November 20, 1989, posted at nepis.epa.gov/Exe/ZyNET. exe/91014F8ZTXT?ZyActionS&BackDesc=Results%ZOpage&Maximum Pages=1&ZyEntry=1&SeekPage=x&yPURL.

32   *"A building properly conceived"*: Stewart Brand, *How Buildings Learn* (New York: Penguin Books, 1994), 12.

32   *"Metal detectors set up at the entrances to schools"*: Donald Barthelme, *Paradise* (New York: Penguin books, 1987), 68.

32   *"virtual snowfall of pale plastic litter"*: John Updike, "Personal Archeology," *New Yorker*, May 29, 2000, 125.

33   *"urgent necessity for any writer"*: Murray, *The Hero and the Blues*, 81.

33    *"We are . . . entrusting to software"*: Birkerts, *Readings*, 53.

33    *"becomes not what happened in it"*: Brand, *How Buildings Learn*, 73, 87.

34    *"from the caves in the lava beds"*: Patricia Limerick, *Something in the Soil* (New York: W. W. Norton & Company, 2000), 33.

34    *"Sometimes the climate of [a particular house]"*: John Cheever, "The Seaside Houses," in *The Collected Stories of John Cheever* (New York: Alfred A. Knopf, 1978), 482–83, 489.

35    *"The sea that morning"*: Cheever, "Goodbye, My Brother," in *The Collected Stories of John Cheever*, 21.

35    *"She was scared"*: Bret Easton Ellis, *American Psycho* (New York: Vintage Contemporaries, 1991), 284.

35    *"When an entire new class"*: Norman Mailer, "Children of the Pied Piper," *Vanity Fair*, March 1991, 159.

36    *"An early morning railroad disaster"*: Cheever, "The Enormous Radio," in *The Collected Stories of John Cheever*, 37.

37    *"The "unexalted kingdom [of the dead]"*: Cheever, "The Death of Justina," in *The Collected Stories of John Cheever*, 437.

37    *"Death is the sanction"*: John Berger, *Keeping a Rendezvous* (New York: Pantheon Books, 1991), 59.


Company

39    *"Because writing can conserve speech"*: Peter Elbow, *Vernacular Eloquence: What Speech Can Bring to Writing* (Oxford: Oxford University Press, 2012), 41.

40    *"vernacular spoken language of his region"*: ibid., 7.

41    *nominalization*: ibid., 82–83.

41    *left-branching, right-branching*: ibid., 85–86.

42    *"intonation units"*: ibid., 109.

43    *"linguistic knowledge"*: ibid., 227–28.


What It Was, What It Could Have Been

46    *"Whereof one cannot speak"*: Ludwig Wittgenstein, *Tractatus Logico-Philosophicus*, trans. C. K. Ogden (1922; New York: Dover, 1999): Proposition 7.

47    *"Harris is . . . attracted"*: Elizabeth McBride, "Tracy Harris," *ARTnews*, December 1991.

47    *"have the appearance"*: Susan Chadwick, "Stunningly Moody Work of Tracy Harris on Exhibit in Graham," *Houston Post*, December 22, 1992.

47   *"turbines, cogs, pulleys"*: Lorraine Adams, "Tracy Harris," *Circa*, Winter
     1994.

47   *"star-riven midnight skies"*: Chadwick, "Stunningly Moody Work."

50   *"audaciously ascetic"*: ibid.

50   *"I think there are two parts to painting"*: Mel Bochner quoted by Tracy
     Harris in my conversation with her. For an exploration of Bochner's
     approach to art, see Jared T. Miller, "Mel Bochner Returns to the Jewish
     Museum," *Tablet*, May 2, 2014, http://www.tabletmag.com/scroll/171361
     /mel-bochner-returns-to-the-jewish-museum.

53   *"deeply moving history"*: Adams, "Tracy Harris."

55   *"touch[ing] everything a dozen times"*: Ludwig Wittgenstein, *Wittgenstein's
     Lectures, Cambridge 1930–1932, from the Notes of John King and Desmond
     Lee* (Oxford: Blackwell, 1980), 24.


The Dying Animal

58   *"smiling or touching their wrists"*: Ron Hansen, *Mariette in Ecstasy* (New
     York: HarperCollins, 1991), 12.

58   *"observe a Great Silence"*: ibid., 24.

59   *"No matter how much you know"*: Philip Roth, *The Dying Animal* (Boston:
     Houghton Mifflin, 2001), 33.

59   *"I'll never forget"*: ibid., 24.

60   *"Consume my heart away"*: W. B. Yeats, "Sailing to Byzantium"; the poem
     can be found at the Academy of American Poets website, http://www.
     poets.org/poetsorg/poem/sailing-byzantium.

60   *"so newly hatched"* and subsequent quotes in this section: Roth, *The Dying
     Animal*, 5, 14, 15.

61   *"I have to go"*: ibid., 156.

62   *"revolution"* and subsequent quotes in this section: ibid., 51, 58–59, 53, 69.

63   *"gorgeous breasts"*: ibid., 5.


Dante's Astronomer

67   *"almost unintelligible"*: T. S. Eliot, "Dante," in *The Sacred Wood* (London:
     Methuen & Company, 1920), 168.

68   *"elevational influence"*: M. A. Evershed and J. Evershed, "Dante and
     Medieval Astronomy," *Journal of the British Astronomical Society*, no. 442
     (December 1911): 440–44.

69   *"small bark"*: Dante, *Purgatorio*, trans. Jean Hollander and Robert
     Hollander (New York: Anchor Books, 2003), 5.

70    *"people (children and adults)"*: Mary T. Bruck, "Mary Ackworth Evershed nee Orr (1867–1949), Solar Physicist and Dante Scholar," *Journal of Astronomical History and Heritage* 1, no. 1 (1998): 45.

70    *"I have not had the opportunity"*: John Tebbut, foreword to M. A. Orr, *An Easy Guide to the Southern Stars* (London: Gall & Inglis, 1897), i.

70    *"pure"*: Dante, *Purgatorio*, 751.

71    *"lights the starry heavens above"*: cited in Barbara Reynolds, "Introduction to the Second Edition" of M. A. Orr, *Dante and the Early Astronomers* (London: Kennikat Press, 1969), 18.

72    *whose name will never be known to us*: speculation has touched on Mary Somerville, Caroline Herschel, and a school teacher named Richard Bloxam, who may have masked himself as a "lady."

73    *"behold . . . floating worlds"*: ibid., 19.

73    *"unfortunate weather"*: Marilyn Bailey Ogilvie, "Obligatory Amateurs: Annie Maunder (1868–1947) and British Women Astronomers at the Dawn of Professional Astronomy," *British Journal of the History of Science* 33 (2000): 78–79.

74    *The papers suggest she traveled with four other women*: Reynolds, "Introduction," 17.

74    *"by a lucky accident"*: F. M. Stratton, "John Evershed, 1864–1956," *Biographical Memoirs of Fellows of the Royal Society* 3 (November 1957): 41.

74    *"The sun was put to shame"*: cited in J. B. Zirker, *Total Eclipses of the Sun* (New York: Van Nostrand Reinhold Company, 1984), 5.

77    *"He / who rules the universe"*: Dante, *Inferno*, trans. Jean Hollander and Robert Hollander (New York: Anchor Books, 2000), 97.

77    *"posterity may be informed"*: M. K. V. Bappu, "The Kodaikanal Observatory—A Historical Account," *Journal of Astrophysical Astronomy* 21 (2000): 103.

78    *"we may never know"*: Willie Wei-Hock Soon and Steven H. Yaskell, *The Maunder Minimum and the Variable Sun-Earth Connection* (Hackensack, N.J.: World Scientific, 2003), 221.

78    *"absorption hypotheses"*: J. Evershed, "The Cause of Darkness in Sunspots," *Astrophysical Journal* 5 (1897): 247.

78    *"relative speed of approach"*: J. Evershed, "Observations of Halley's Comet," *Kodaikanal Bulletin*, no. 20 (June 22, 1910): 199–207.

78    *"Day after day, sitting quietly"*: John Evershed and Mary Ackworth Evershed, *Memoirs of the Kodaikanal Observatory: Results of Prominence Observations* (Kodaikanal: Government Press, 1917), 55.

79    *"It is a matter of regret"*: Edward Moore, "The Astronomy of Dante," in *Studies in Dante*, 3rd ser. (Oxford: Oxford University Press, 1903 [1968]), 1.

80   *"Midway along the journey of our life"*: Dante, *Inferno*, 3.

80   *He is named directly—just once*: see Dante, *Purgatorio*, 669.

80   *"trees on earth"*: ibid.

80   *"heaven of the fish"*: Moore, "The Astronomy of Dante," 55.

80   *"This amounts to saying"*: ibid., 106.

81   *Mary wrote that the lunar circles of Ptolemy*: Evershed and Evershed, "Dante and Medieval Astronomy," 440–44.

81   *"mirror of the sun"*: cited in Orr, *Dante and the Early Astronomers*, 182.

82   *"problem[s]"* and subsequent quotes in this section: Evershed and Evershed, *Dante and the Early Astronomers*, 288, 312–16, 149, 168, 172, 175, 270, 330.

84   *"not a single northern spot has been seen"*: Bappu, "The Kodaikanal Observatory," 57–58.

84   *"No one will dispute a poet's right"* and subsequent quotes in this section: Bruck, "Mary Ackworth Evershed," 54–55.

85   *"to study the history of astronomy"*: ibid., 55.

86   *"much occupied"*: J. Evershed, "Recollections of Seventy Years of Scientific Work," *Vistas in Astronomy* 1 (1955), 36, 38.

86   *"However ill"*: Stratton, "John Evershed, 1864–1956," 48.

86   *"From then on, I was able to explain"*: Bruck, "Mary Ackworth Evershed": 56.

86   *"sealed book"*: Barbara Reynolds, *The Passionate Intellect: Dorothy L. Sayers' Encounters with Dante* (Kent: Kent State University Press, 1989), 117, 225.

86   *"unjustly neglected"*: Colin Hardie, Review of *Dante and the Early Astronomers*, *Modern Language Review* 52, no. 4 (1957): 614.

87   *"phase of culture"*: Reynolds, "Introduction," 20.

87   *"unbelievably apt and accurate"*: Mark A. Peterson. "Dante and the 3-Sphere," *American Journal of Physics* 47, no. 12 (1979): 1031–35.

87   *"love . . . governs heaven"*: Alison Cornish, *Reading Dante's Stars* (New Haven: Yale University Press, 2000), 10.


Silent Screams

88   "*After my death no one will find*": Søren Kierkegaard, *Papers and Journals: A Selection*, ed. and trans. Alastair Hannay (London: Penguin Books, 1996), 154–55.

88   "*Kierkegaard knew very well how matters stood*": Franz Kafka, diary excerpts in *Dearest Father: Stories and Other Writings*, trans. Ernst Kaiser and Eithene Wilkin (New York: Shocken Books, 1954), 101–103.

88   *According to Mark C. Taylor*: Mark C. Taylor, *Tears* (Albany: State University of New York Press, 1990), 174.

89   *"Dearest Father"*: Franz Kafka, "Letter to His Father," in *Dearest Father*, 138.

89   *"spiritual poverty"*: Franz Kafka, *Dearest Father*, 102–3.

89   *"If we read* The Scream*"*: Taylor, *Tears*, 176.

90   *"by bypassing"*: Donald Barthelme, "Interview with Charles Ruas and Judith Sherman, 1975," in *Not-Knowing: The Essays and Interviews*, ed. Kim Herzinger (New York: Random House, 1997), 221.

90   *"despised"*: Hubert Benoit, *The Many Faces of Love*, trans. P. Mairet (London: Routledge and Kegan Paul, 1955), 150.

90   *"Do I want to be loved"*: Donald Barthelme, "Rebecca," in *Sixty Stories* (New York: Putnam, 1981), 284.


Mr. Either and Mr. Or

91   *"a man of wit and taste"*: Jean-François de Bastide, *The Little House: An Architectural Seduction*, trans. Rodolphe el-Khoury (Princeton: Princeton University Press, 1996), 57, 58.

92   *"Your despair is my delight"*: ibid., 65, 66, 67.

95   *"during the atmospheric testing era"*: Carole Gallagher, *American Ground Zero: The Secret Nuclear War* (New York: Random House, 1993), 310.

95   *"When a man is asleep"*: Marcel Proust, *Swann's Way*, trans. C. K. Scott Moncreif (New York: Modern Library, 1956), 25.

97   *writers like Diderot and Voltaire*: Rodolphe el-Khoury, "Architecture in the Bedroom," introduction to de Bastide, *The Little House*, 38.

97   *"odorless paint"*: de Bastide, *The Little House*: 72.

98   *"Once upon a time"*: Søren Kierkegaard, *Fear and Trembling*, trans. Alastair Hannay (New York: Penguin Books, 1985), 44, 71, 46.

99   *"Our social personality"*: Proust, *Swann's Way*, 116–17.

99   *"Whatever shall hap[pen]"*: William Shakespeare, *Hamlet*, in *The Riverside Shakespeare*, ed. G. Blakemore Evans (Boston: Houghton Mifflin Company, 1974), 1146.

100   *"When I saw any external object"*: Proust, *Swann's Way*, 90.

100   *"Method and object cannot be separated"*: Werner Heisenberg, cited in Patrick A. Heelin, *Quantum Mechanics and Objectivity: A Study of the Physical Philosophy of Werner Heisenberg* (New York: Springer, 2012), 153.

A Pigeon Coop, a Crystal Palace

103 *"No ideas but in things"*: William Carlos Williams, *Paterson* (1963; repr. New York: Penguin Books, 1983), 6.

107 *"The man who makes a thing that moves"*: William Gass, "Philosophy and the Form of Fiction," in *Fiction and the Figures of Life* (Boston: David R. Godine, 1971), 9.

110 *"When I think about Abraham"* and subsequent quotes in this section: Søren Kierkegaard, *Fear and Trembling*, trans. Alistair Hannay (New York: Penguin books, 1985), 62, 63, 68–69, 44.

112 *"I am a sick man"*: Fyodor Dostoevsky, *Notes from Underground* trans. Richard Pevear and Larissa Volokhonksy (New York: Vintage Books, 1993), 1.

112 *"Such persons"*: ibid., prefatory note.

112 *"I was conscious"*: ibid., 5.

114 *"That's the idea"*: Samuel Beckett, *Waiting for Godot* (1952; repr., New York: Grove Press, 1982), 219–20.

114 *"Charming evening we're having"*: ibid., 111.

114 *free indirect speech*: David Lodge, *Consciousness and the Novel: Connected Essays* (Cambridge, Mass.: Harvard University Press, 2002), 37.

115 *"Cinderella inquired"*: ibid.

115 *"Was that the clock"*: ibid.

115 *"The leaves of the tree"*: Ernest Hemingway, "A Clean, Well-lighted Place," in *The Complete Short Stories of Ernest Hemingway: The Finca Vigia Edition* (New York: Simon & Schuster, 2002), 288.

115 *Biographer Ronald Hayman*: Ronald Hayman, *Sartre: A Life* (New York: Simon & Schuster, 1987), 97–98.

116 *"Its presence pressed itself"*: Jean-Paul Sartre, *Nausea*, trans. Lloyd Alexander (New York: New directions, 1964), 127–28.

116 *"What is more abstract"*: Randall Jarrell, cited in Daniel Albright, *Beckett and Aesthetics* (Cambridge: Cambridge University Press, 2003), 131–32.

117 *"The light grows softer"*: Sartre, *Nausea*, 53.

Writing Political Fiction

121 *"war was always there"*: Ernest Hemingway, "In Another Country," in *The Complete Short Stories of Ernest Hemingway* (New York: Scribner's, 1998), 206.

122 *"poetry is the spontaneous overflow of powerful feeling"*: William Wordsworth, "Observations Prefixed to *Lyrical Ballads* [1802]," in *Prefaces and Prologues to Famous Books: The Harvard Classics Series*, vol. 39, ed. Charles W. Eliot (New York: P. F. Collier and Sons, 1909–14), 26.

122    *"write . . . as if you were already dead"*: Susan Gardner, "A Story for This
Time and Place: An Interview with Nadine Gordimer about *Burger's
Daughter*," in *Nadine Gordimer's Burger's Daughter: A Casebook*, ed. Judie
Newman (New York: Oxford University Press, 2003), 30.

125    *"So with the lamps all put out"* and subsequent quotes in this section:
Virginia Woolf, *To the Lighthouse* (1927; repr., New York: Harcourt, 2005),
129–30, 131, 138, 149.


American Speech, American Silence

127    *"enjoying the fellowship"* and all other quotes from Edward Kennedy's
testimony and the Chappaquiddick investigation and findings: James A.
Boyle, *Inquest into the Death of Mary Jo Kopechne* (Edgartown, Mass.:
Edgartown District Court OCLC 180774589, 1970.

128    *"She didn't drown"*: Edward Klein, *Ted Kennedy: The Dream That Never
Died* (New York: Crown, 2009), 93.

129    *"We figured that people would think"*: Nellie Bly, *The Kennedy Men: Three
Generations of Sex, Scandal, and Secrets* (New York: Kensington Books,
1996), 216.

129    *"decay"* and subsequent quotes in this section: Joyce Carol Oates, *Black
Water* (New York: Dutton, 1992), 8, 7, 5, 21, 18, 36, 26, 31, 46, 60–61.

130    *"Jeffersonian Idealism"* and subsequent quotes in this section: ibid., 12,
139, 85, 13, 44, 32.

131    *"had been talking companionably together"* and subsequent quotes in this
section: ibid., 5, 145, 11, 49.

132    *"should be like a beacon"*: Joseph Conrad, "Heart of Darkness," in *The
Collected Tales of Joseph Conrad*, ed. Samuel Hynes (New York: Ecco
Press, 1992), 35.

133    *"the key to America's future salvation"*: Oates, *Black Water*, 41.

133    *"It might be argued"* and other quotes from Joyce Carol Oates's now
inaccessible *Guardian* essay on Ted Kennedy from August 2009: see
"Joyce Carol Oates on Teddy Kennedy," in *For What It's Worth*, a blog by
Christopher Fountain, August 28, 2009, http://www.christopherfountain.
com/2009/08/28/joyce-carol-oates-on-ted-kennedy/; and "Joyce Carol
Oates on Teddy Kennedy," *Celestial Timepiece: A Joyce Carol Oates
Patchwork*, August 6, 009, http://www.celestialtimepiece.com/2009/08/26
/joyce-carol-oates-on-ted-kennedy.

134    *"shallow ditch"*: Oates, *Black Water*, 9.

134    *"a broken dinette table"*: ibid., 149.

134    *"Not now, not like this"*: ibid., 9.

The Black Butterfly

135   *"Making love with your socks on"*: Gabriel García Márquez, *Gabriel García Márquez: The Last Interview and Other Conversations*, ed. David Streitfeld (Brooklyn: Melville House, 2015). This line appears originally in an interview conducted by Alonso Angel Restrepo entitled "A Novelist Who Will Keep Writing Novels" (as translated by Theo Ellin Ballew), originally published in 1956 in *El Columbiano Literaria*. It is unpaginated in the Melville House reprint.

135   *"Because Cortes lands"*: Donald Barthelme, "Cortés and Montezuma," in *Great Days* (New York: Farrar, Straus, & Giroux, 1979), 41.

136   *"Many people coincided"*: Gabriel García Márquez, *Chronicle of a Death Foretold*, trans. Gregory Rabassa (New York: Alfred A. Knopf, 1983), 4, 17.

137   *"merriment"* and subsequent quotes in this section: Machado de Assis, *Epitaph of a Small Winner*, trans. William L. Grossman (1952; repr. New York: Farrar, Straus, & Giroux, 1998), 5, 67, 98, 97, 91, 118.

138   *"face"* and subsequent quotes in this section: García Márquez, *Chronicle of a Death Foretold*, 9, 15, 13, 48, 72, 76.

140   *"the main defect of this book"*: de Assis, *Epitaph of a Small Winner*, 117.


The Babies in the Room

141   *"Journey of Self-Discovery"*: first published in "News in Brief," *The Onion*, February 10, 2011.

142   *"You're starting to think"*: first published in "Horoscopes," *The Onion*, September 28, 2010.


Mother

149   *"Just this morning"*: Grace Paley, *Enormous Changes at the Last Minute* (New York: Farrar, Straus, & Giroux, 1974), 5.

149   *"I want . . . to be a different person"*: ibid.

150   *"I forget the names of my friends"* and subsequent quotes in this section: Grace Paley, *Fidelity* (New York: Farrar, Straus, & Giroux, 2008), 5.

151   *"One day I was listening to the AM radio"* and subsequent quotes in this section: Grace Paley, *Later the Same Day* (New York: Farrar, Straus, & Giroux, 1985), 111–12.


The Tragic Necessity of Human Life

154   *"I don't have a story"*: Grace Paley, public interview at Oregon State University, "An Evening with Grace Paley," January 30, 1996.

154   *"I first met Myra Henshawe"* and subsequent quotes in this section: Willa Cather, *My Mortal Enemy*, in *Stories, Poems, and Other Writings*, ed. Sharon O'Brien (New York: The Library of America, 1992), 533, 539, 552, 558.

155   *"sprawling overgrown west-coast city"* and subsequent quotes in this section: ibid., 559, 564.

155   *"The novel, for a long while, has been overfurnished"*: Willa Cather, "The Novel Démeublé," in *Stories, Poems, and Other Writings*, 834.

155   *"Is the story of a banker"*: ibid., 835.

156   *"stage people"*: Cather, *My Mortal Enemy*, 554.

156   *"most . . . are dead now"*: ibid.

157   *"Nobody can paint the sun"*: Willa Cather, "Light on Adobe Walls," in *Stories, Poems, and Other Writings*, 976.

157   *"Whatever is felt upon the page"*: Cather, "The Novel Démeublé," 837.

157   *"violent nature"*: Cather, *My Mortal Enemy*, 577.

157   *"Human relationships are the tragic necessity"*: Willa Cather, "Katharine Mansfield," in *Stories, Poems, and Other Writings*, 878.

157   *"In many of them"*: Willa Cather, "On *The Professor's House*" in *Stories, Poems, and Other Writings*, 974.

158   *"in some lonely and unfrequented place"*: Cather, *My Mortal Enemy*, 580.


Perhaps America

159   *"My feet are cold and wet"*: Kim Townsend, *Sherwood Anderson* (Boston: Houghton Mifflin Company, 1987), 77.

161   *"What was a fellow to do?"*: Sherwood Anderson, *Dark Laughter* (New York: Grosset & Dunlap, 1926), 22, 18.

162   *"Love-making was after all a symbol"*: Sherwood Anderson, *Many Marriages* (Metuchen, N.J.: Scarecrow Press, 1978), 217.

163   *"As to what happened downstairs"*: Sherwood Anderson, "The Egg," in *Sherwood Anderson: Short Stories*, ed. Maxwell Geismar (New York: Hill & Wang, 1962), 27, 30.

163   *"I'm just trying to make you understand"*: Sherwood Anderson, "The Man Who Became a Woman," in *Sherwood Anderson: Short Stories:*, 73.

164   *"Miss Stein is a worker in words"*: Sherwood Anderson, *Sherwood Anderson's Notebook* (New York: Boni & Liveright, 1926), 48.

164   *"Consider the tantalizing difference"*: Anderson, *Sherwood Anderson's Notebook*, 31.

166   *"I'm not any fairy"*: Anderson, "The Man Who Became a Woman," in *Sherwood Anderson: Short Stories*, 73.

166  *"American men"*: Sherwood Anderson, *The Letters of Sherwood Anderson*, ed. Howard Mumford Jones (New York: Little Brown, 1953), 153–54.

166  *"The Mississippi River"*: Anderson, *Sherwood Anderson's Notebook*, 225.

167  *"There was a cleansing"*: Sherwood Anderson, *Many Marriages* (New York: B. W. Huebsch, Inc., 1923), 189.

167  *"'Oh,' I thought"*: Ray Lewis White, ed., *Sherwood Anderson's Memoirs: A Critical Edition* (Chapel Hill: University of North Carolina Press, 1969), 249.

167  *Lucile and Jerry Blum*: Anderson, *The Letters of Sherwood Anderson*, 67–69.

168  *His next letter*: ibid.

168  *"I would like to write the story of a man"*: Sherwood Anderson, cited in Jon S. Lawry, "'Death in the Woods' and the Artist's Self in Sherwood Anderson," *PMLA* 74, no. 3 (1959): 306.

169  *"I am in the position of many writers"*: Sherwood Anderson, *Puzzled America* (Mamaroneck, N.Y.: Paul P. Appel, 1970), ix.

169  *"In the mill"*: Sherwood Anderson. *Beyond Desire* (New York: Liveright, 1932), 72.

170  *"You see, the writer wants to explain himself"*: Anderson, *Sherwood Anderson's Notebook*: 30–31.

Afterword

171  *"Fail. Fail again"*: Samuel Beckett, "Three Dialogues," in *Disjecta*, ed. Ruby Cohn (New York: Grove Press, 1984), 142.

171  *"Nothing to paint"*: ibid.

171  *"What an artist does is fail"*: Donald Barthelme, "The Sandman," in *Sadness* (New York: Farrar, Straus, & Giroux, 1972), 93.

171  *"not-knowing"*: Donald Barthelme, "Not-Knowing," in *Not-Knowing: The Essays and Interviews*, ed. Kim Herzinger (New York: Vintage International, 1997), 12.

172  *"Is whispering nothing?"*: William Shakespeare, *The Winter's Tale*, in *The Riverside Shakespeare*, ed. G. Blakemore Evans (Boston: Houghton Mifflin Company, 1974), 1573.

173  *thick ticking of the tin clock*: Bernard Malamud, "Idiots First," in *The Complete Stories*, ed. Robert Giroux (New York: Farrar, Straus, & Giroux, 1997), 273.

174  *"The crowd at the ball game"*: William Carlos Williams, "At the Ball Game," in *The Selected Poems* (New York: New Directions, 1969), 31.